BRIGHT

NEW IDEAS

Drama and Role-play

AGES 5-11

Nichola Rees

Author
Nichola Rees

Editor
Frances Ridley

Assistant editor
Jennifer Shiels

Project editor
Wendy Tse

Series designer
Joy Monkhouse

Designers
Eric Ivens
Melissa Leeke

Illustrations
Garry Davies

Cover photographs
© 2005 Comstock Inc

Published by Scholastic Ltd,
Book End,
Range Road,
Whitney,
Oxfordshire
OX29 0YD

Printed by Bell & Bain Ltd, Glasgow
Text © Nichola Rees 2005
© 2005 Scholastic Ltd
6 7 8 9 0   0 1 2 3 4

Mixed Sources
Product group from well-managed
forests and other controlled sources
www.fsc.org Cert no. TT-COC-002769
© 1996 Forest Stewardship Council
FSC

Visit our website at www.scholastic.co.uk

British Library Cataloguing-in-Publication Data
A catalogue record for this book is available from
the British Library.

ISBN 0-439-96503-9
ISBN 978-0439-96503-3

Material from the National Curriculum
© The Queen's Printer and Controller of
HMSO. Reproduced under the terms of
HMSO Guidance Note 8.
Material from the NNS and NLS © Crown
Copyright. Reproduced under the terms of
HMSO Guidance Note 8.

Contents

Chapter 5 – Music

Chapter 6 – Religious education

Chapter 7 – Physical education

Chapter 8 – Information and communication technology

Drama and Role-play

Introduction

Welcome to *Bright Ideas: Drama and Role-play*. This book provides a rich collection of activities that integrate drama with different National Curriculum subject areas. Drama can make the teaching and learning of a subject more enjoyable and help to improve children's understanding. The games in this book are both mentally and physically stimulating, and they demonstrate that, above all, drama and learning can be fun!

Drama in the National Curriculum

Although drama is not a separate curriculum subject at primary level, teaching drama is a statutory requirement of the National Curriculum for English under the heading of 'Speaking and Listening' (En1). The Programme of Study for English requires children to participate in a range of drama activities by: working in role; presenting drama and stories (Key Stage 1); scripting and performing plays (Key Stage 2); responding to performances. The role-play activities in this book enable the children to think carefully about the use of appropriate language to convey situations and character, to work individually and with others, and to consider the effectiveness of different dramatic techniques, such as creating tableaux, narration, improvisation and role-play. Drama and role-play are invaluable in providing alternative ways in which children can relate to a subject and in developing their self-confidence.

This book provides the drama objectives outlined in the Programme of Study for English, rather than the specific drama guidelines covered by the *Speaking, Listening and Learning handbook*. Because the activities can be used across different age ranges, it is best to fit the activity to the abilities of the children, so more able children may be given more freedom to develop their own scripts, while less able children may need more adult support or would benefit from working in mixed-ability groups.

Using this book

Drama and Role-play is accessible and easy to use. It has eight chapters, each dealing with a different subject area. Each activity aims to develop understanding and learning in each particular subject and to develop confidence and empathy skills through drama, role-play and performance. A suggested age range, curriculum links and a list of resources are given at the beginning of each activity.

The subjects covered are history, geography, science, art and design, music, religious education, physical education and information and communication technology. The activities cater for children across the primary age range, from five- to eleven-years-old. Some of the activities are accompanied by photocopiable sheets, which are grouped at the end of each chapter.

Through the different subject areas, various dramatic techniques and forms can be taught. The activities will introduce the children to interviewing, creating tableaux and sketches, improvising, devising monologues and dialogues, creating characters, writing plays, composing songs for performance and devising TV programmes. All these activities focus on developing communication skills and self-confidence through role-play and performance. The children are encouraged to work both independently and in groups, and there are activities that will suit all, from the timid to the exuberant child. In each of the activities the children should always support and listen to each other's performances politely.

Many of the skills that can be developed via drama and role-play, such as empathy, storytelling and performance, can be used to build on the narrative aspects of subjects such as history and religious education. For example, in the activity 'Newscasters' (Chapter 1 – History), children 'interview' eye-witnesses of the Great Fire of London. Drama can also be a valuable teaching tool to enhance subject knowledge and understanding, for example, by physically re-enacting certain events or phenomena. In the activity 'Current' (Chapter 3 – Science), children learn about the importance of an unbroken circuit by physically imitating an electric current.

Basic speaking and listening skills are developed through many of the activities as the children are encouraged to speak clearly and with confidence, as well as to listen and respond to the performances of others. The nature of drama and role-play also means that the children are taught to interact and work well in groups, and to discuss ideas together when planning short sketches or tableaux. The children should all be encouraged to contribute and to listen to each other when working in groups.

The activities require very little preparation and are easy to integrate into current planning. In the most demanding cases, you may need a bigger space. You may also need to prepare photocopies or assemble a few props. Good preparation in the subject area is important. Although two objectives, one for the subject and one for drama, have been given for each activity, the assumption is that the subject in question has been covered by the class. The emphasis of the activities is on exploring the subject through drama.

The 66 activities provided by this book are flexible and many can be easily adapted to suit different age ranges and ranges of ability. The activities also vary: some are quite short while others will require more time; some are very physical while others are mental. The ages and abilities of children in your class will also affect how much time you give to an activity and how much support you offer. The 'Differentiation' section in each activity gives some guidance on how you can support less able children and stretch more able children.

Bright Ideas: Drama and Role-play is a practical and flexible resource. It can be used with all age ranges and at differing academic levels, and will help you to introduce fresh and creative ideas into your classroom.

CHAPTER 1

History

AGE RANGE 5–7

LEARNING OBJECTIVES
To gain confidence by speaking in front of an audience; to look at how famous people from the past gained their reputation.

CURRICULUM LINKS
History KS1: 1a, 2a, 5, 6c.
QCA History: Unit 4 – Why do we remember Florence Nightingale?

Question and answer

What you need
Safe open space; mock microphone; whiteboard or flipchart; pens; paper; pencils.

What to do
● Gather the children together in a circle so that they are sitting comfortably, with their hands in their laps. Sit in front of them in the same position.
● Ask the children if they know what the word 'interview' means. Ask them to think of any examples of interviews they have seen, and to describe what they remember.
● Explain to the children that the aim of an interview is to find out information from someone.
● Group the children in pairs, giving each pair a piece of paper and a pencil.
● Ask the children to imagine that they are going to interview Florence Nightingale.
● Write a series of questions on the board that the children would like to ask her, concentrating on Florence's profession as a nurse during the Crimean War. For example, *What is it like being a nurse? Why do you do it? What qualities do you think make a good nurse? How many hours a day do you work? What effect has the war had on you?* and so on.
● Encourage them to ask questions that will find out information rather than yes/no questions.
● Ask the children to write down the answers to the questions that they are going to ask Florence Nightingale on their pieces of paper. For example, *Being a nurse is very difficult as you have to work very long hours and sometimes you don't have enough medicine to help everyone.* Write down key words or phrases on the board if they need prompts.
● Ask the group to give examples of some of their questions and answers.
● When you are satisfied with their questions and answers, invite them to devise a mock interview of what happens between themselves and Florence Nightingale.
● Encourage the children to work in their pairs to devise a maximum of eight questions and to place them in order of importance, question one being the most important and question eight being the least. Explain to the children that sometimes not all questions can be asked in an interview, so it is important to ask the good ones first.
● When you think that the pairs are ready, ask them to deliver their interview to the rest of the group, using the mock microphone as a prop.
● As each pair finishes, give the two children marks out of ten for their delivery.

Differentiation
You may need to give younger children help with the questions and answers. Ask more confident children to take on a persona, by thinking about the character of the reporter or of Florence Nightingale.

By the seaside

AGE RANGE 5–7

LEARNING OBJECTIVES
To learn the importance of stillness and expression in drama; to think about the differences between life in the past and present.

CURRICULUM LINKS
History KS1: 2b, 4a, 5.
QCA History: Unit 3 – What were seaside holidays like in the past?

What you need
Safe, open space; selection of photographs or pictures representing beach holidays in the past and present.

What to do
● Ask the children to sit in a large circle.
● Place your selection of pictures of beach holidays during different decades in the centre of the circle.
● Ask the children to spend a couple of minutes studying the images.
● Encourage the children to explain what they see in the pictures. Listen to some of the children's interpretations, and invite comments and suggestions from others.
● Ask the children to support their opinions with evidence from the pictures, for example, *The swimming costumes are very different from what they are like today.*
● Prompt the children to compare beach holidays now to what they think beach holidays were like 20 years ago (or longer, if you have copies of older images).
● After discussion, divide the children into groups of five or six. Allocate a leader for each group.
● Ask each leader to choose two differing pictures. Make sure that there is an obvious difference in their choices, to encourage the children to think about a wider range of characters and periods.
● The leaders then show their groups the photographs. One of the photographs is selected, and the leader gives members of the group a character to imitate.
● Once the children have been allocated their characters, they have to choose a name and work out what their relationship is to the rest of the characters in the photograph. For example, *My name is Jack, I am six and I'm playing with my older sister.*
● The children should practise copying the image of the photographs that they are working on, to make still-life versions of them.
● When you are happy that each group has the right idea, ask them to perform their tableaux to the rest of the class. At the end of each performance, encourage the children to step out of character one at a time and explain who they are in relation to the picture.
● Encourage the rest of the group to ask questions about the different characters.
● Then invite the children to repeat the process for the second photograph. Ask them to think about how the two photographs are different, and to discuss this among themselves. How can they bring out the differences in the way they perform the tableau?

Differentiation
With older children, choose photographs or pictures that are more interesting. Get them to concentrate on their characters' histories and the current mood they are in. Encourage the children to explore their characters in depth.

Drama and Role-play

AGE RANGE 8–9

LEARNING OBJECTIVES
To look at the lives of people in Tudor times; to realise the importance of status in Tudor times; to think about how status can be conveyed in drama, through gesture and expression.

CURRICULUM LINKS
History KS2: 2a, 2b, 3, 10.
QCA History: Unit 8 – What were the differences between the lives of rich and poor people in Tudor times?

Please sir!

What you need
Safe, open space; OHP; 'Please sir!' photocopiable page 17 made into an OHT.

What to do
● Place the 'Please sir!' OHT on the OHP. Ask the children to look at the four different cartoons, which are all set in Tudor times. Each scenario revolves around status, for example, in the first cartoon a rich business man is leaving a shop and a street urchin asks him for some change.
● Ask the children to describe what they see in the cartoons and if they have an idea as to what kind of story is taking place.
● Challenge the children to spot the differences between the characters in the cartoons. (Each cartoon contrasts characters of very high and very low status.) Ask the children to think about the clothes that the people are wearing and what they are doing in the pictures.
● Ask for volunteers to highlight to the rest of the class the differences that they can see in the pictures.
● Explain to the children what the word 'status' means. Tell them that in Tudor times, people who were rich had 'high status' and people who were poor had 'low status'.

● Ask the children to stand up and to create a still character of 'low status', concentrating on what their bodies look like. Ask them to imagine what their clothes would be like. Would the character be cold? Hot? Comfortable?
● When you are satisfied that the children have understood the task, ask them to create a character of 'high status', while you repeat the same questions.
● Encourage the children to elaborate on what kind of a person would have 'high status' and what kind of person would have 'low status' in Tudor times. Ask them to give examples.
● Group the children into pairs, asking the members of each pair to label themselves 'A' and 'B'. Person A is to be someone of 'high status' during Tudor times, and person B is to be someone of 'low status' during Tudor times.
● Ask the pairs to pick one of the four cartoons from the OHT. They should then devise a sketch based upon it, concentrating on status. Encourage them to think about dialogue and interaction between the two characters.
● When the children have finished devising and rehearsing, invite them to perform their sketches to the rest of the class.

Differentiation
Encourage older children to work on their characterisation by concentrating on posture and speech.

 BRIGHT IDEAS Drama and Role-play

AGE RANGE 8–11

LEARNING OBJECTIVES
To learn the importance of storytelling in drama; to imagine what life was like in the court of Henry VIII.

CURRICULUM LINKS
History KS1 and KS2: 2a, 5, 10.
QCA History: Unit 7 – Why did Henry VIII marry six times?

Rumour chain

What you need
Safe, open space; 'Rumour chain' photocopiable page 18 (one copy for each pair of children).

What to do
● Group the children into pairs.
● Give each pair a copy of the 'Rumour chain' photocopiable sheet and look at the pictures together.
● Explain that the pictures show a story becoming exaggerated. In pairs, ask the children to discuss what is happening in each picture. Listen to some of their interpretations, and invite comments and suggestions from others.
● Ask the children to define what the words 'gossip' and 'exaggerate' mean.
● Encourage the children to support their opinions with evidence from the pictures, such as the characters' facial expression, stance and position.
● After discussion, ask each pair to prepare a scenario between two of Henry VIII's servants. The servants can be located in the kitchen or in Henry VIII's private quarters. The discussion is about his forthcoming wedding to Anne Boleyn, and the servants are to discuss what they think of Anne Boleyn and her demands on them as servants.

● Once you are satisfied that the children are clear about what they have to do, give them five minutes of rehearsal time.
● Watch some of the performances. Ask the rest of the class to offer their opinions on the realism of the dialogue.
● Ask one of the pairs to perform their scenario again, and use it as a starting point for a 'rumour circle'. Call the children Servant 1 and 2, with Servant 1 starting the rumour. When they have finished their scenario, ask Servant 1 to sit down, and invite another child to play Servant 3. Servant 2 then repeats the rumour to Servant 3, but slightly exaggerates some of the information. Servant 2 then exits, to be replaced by Servant 4. Servant 3 continues the rumour, now even more exaggerated.
● Continue this for a maximum of ten servants. Invite constructive comments from the rest of the class.

Differentiation
Allow younger children to write down their opening lines to give them confidence to continue without a script. Challenge older children to experiment with characters and content, giving more realism to their characters.

Drama and Role-play

AGE RANGE 8–11

LEARNING OBJECTIVES
To learn the importance of interview techniques in drama; to learn the importance of asking and answering relevant questions in historical enquiry.

CURRICULUM LINKS
History KS1 and KS2: 4a, 4b, 5, 13.
QCA History: Unit 10 – What can we find out about Ancient Egypt from what has survived?

Discovery

What you need
Safe, open space; two chairs; pens; paper.

What to do
● Gather the children together so that they are sitting comfortably.
● Ask them what they know about Ancient Egypt. Encourage them to talk about the kings and queens who ruled the country, and the treasures and palaces they owned.
● Explain that an archaeologist is someone who studies how people lived in the past. The archaeologist's job involves excavating (digging and exploring) sites and studying physical remains, such as remains of buildings or objects. Encourage the children to share their experiences of archaeology. Talk about real people or characters in films or books, who have similar occupations (for example, Indiana Jones).
● Listen to what the children say, keeping them on focused on the job of an archaeologist.
● Group the children into pairs and ask them to label themselves 'A' and 'B'. Person A is to play an interviewer and person B is to play a famous archaeologist.
● Ask the children to prepare a television interview between the famous archaeologist and the interviewer. The archaeologist has recently found a famous Egyptian treasure that has been lost for thousands of years, for example, a vase belonging to Tutankhamun.
● Ask the pairs to sit down and work together to write a list of questions that the interviewer will ask the archaeologist. Encourage the interviewer to ask interesting questions, such as *Where did you find the vase? How long have you been looking? Did you have any clues as to where to look?* and so on.
● When the children have devised their questions, tell them that you want them to rehearse their interviews. Remind the children that it is important that they create a history for their character and that they should think about what the character looks and sounds like.
● Allow them ten minutes of rehearsal time.
● When the children have finished rehearsing their scenes, ask them to sit quietly on the floor.
● Set up two chairs at the front of the class and inform the children that this is a television studio and that their scenes will be performed on the chairs.
● Invite each pair of children to perform their interviews on the two chairs. The rest of the class plays the audience. At the end of each interview, invite constructive comments from the rest of the class.

Differentiation
Allow younger children to write down opening questions. Less able children may not be confident about making the object up. If so, provide pictures of Egyptian artefacts so that they can pretend that these are the objects they have found. Ask older children to concentrate on characterisation and encourage them to think of more in-depth questions.

Drama and
Role-play

Newscasters

AGE RANGE 7–11

LEARNING OBJECTIVES
To learn the importance of delivery and listening in drama; to think about what it must have been like to have witnessed or experienced the Great Fire of London.

CURRICULUM LINKS
History KS2: 1a, 4b, 5a, 5c, 10.
QCA History: Unit 5 – How do we know about the Great Fire of London?

What you need
Safe, open space; 'The Great Fire of London' photocopiable page 19 (one copy for each member of the class).

What to do
● Gather the children together in a circle so that they are sitting comfortably. Sit in front of them, in the same position, and hand them each a copy of 'The Great Fire of London' photocopiable sheet.

● Ask the children if they watch any news programmes. If the children are too young to watch the news, ask them if they have come across the children's programme 'Newsround'. Do they know what the word 'news' means?

● Encourage the children to elaborate on what they have seen, supporting their examples with subject matter if possible. Use their examples to introduce the concept of an 'eyewitness'.

● Divide the children into two groups.

● Ask the first group to imagine that they are news reporters during the Great Fire of London. Encourage them, in pairs, to think of suitable questions to ask people during that time, for example, *What has happened to you? What has happened to your home as a result of the fire? Where will you live from now on?* and so on. Encourage them to ask

questions to find out information, such as *Where did the fire start? How did it start?* The children can record their questions on the photocopiable sheet.

● Ask the second group to imagine that they are people who have experienced the Great Fire of London in some way. Encourage them to think about the different types of people who lived at this time. How did the rich live? What was life like for the poor? Invite the children to give examples. Ask them to write down a plotted history of their character on the photocopiable sheet. What do they do for a living? How old are they? How have they been affected by the Great Fire?

● When you are satisfied that both groups have fulfilled their tasks, match each news reporter with a character and ask them to prepare an eyewitness interview.

● When the children are ready, ask them to perform the interview to the rest of the group as a live news broadcast from an area near the Great Fire of London.

● Take the role of the anchor newsreader so that the class can switch smoothly between different interviews.

● At the end of each improvisation, invite constructive criticism from the rest of the class.

Differentiation
Allow younger children to use the information on their pieces of paper as prompts. Older students should work without prompts, and their characters and situations should be more defined.

Drama and Role-play

AGE RANGE 8–9

LEARNING OBJECTIVES
To create a character and talk about it for a minute without interruption; to compare the lives of children today with those of children in the Second World War.

CURRICULUM LINKS
History KS2: 2a, 11b.
QCA History: Unit 9 – What was it like for children in the Second World War?

Tell my story

What you need
'Tell my story' photocopiable page 20 (one copy for each member of the class); whiteboard or flipchart; pens; chair; paper; pencils; stopwatch.

What to do
● Gather the children together and sit them in a large circle.
● Ask the children what they know about the Second World War. Do they have any interesting information that they could share with the rest of the group?
● Encourage them to give evidence and examples that they have seen, heard or experienced.
● Write a list on the board with two headings: 'Present' and 'The Second World War'.
● Ask the children to think about the daily activities of children during the Second World War and how they would be different compared to today's activities, for example, children during the Second World War would not have had so many toys to play with, but they would have had much more freedom to play outside in the street or surrounding countryside.
● When you are satisfied that the list is long enough, hand each child a copy of 'Tell my story'.
● Ask the children to imagine that they are living during the Second World War. To help them do this, ask them to fill in the copy of 'Tell my story' and to draw a picture of what they think their character looks like.
● Encourage the children to think about wartime restrictions. For example, they may like to eat chocolate but it was rationed during the war and was considered a rare luxury.
● When the children have completed the task, ask them to try and memorise some of the information they have written, as they will shortly 'become' that character.
● Encourage the children to work on their own for five minutes to prepare a one-minute monologue, based on the information they have devised.
● When they are ready, ask them to put their pens and paper down and to sit quietly.
● Invite the children to take turns to come to the front of the class, sit on the chair provided and deliver their monologue.
● Using a stopwatch, hold a competition and challenge them to talk in character about their life during the Second World War for one minute or longer if they are able.

Differentiation
Keep to the one-minute limit for less able children. When working with older children, give them more time to work on their characterisation. They could take on the roles of evacuees and talk about their experiences, and the differences between life in the country and city.

Drama and
Role-play

Who's better off?

AGE RANGE 9–11

LEARNING OBJECTIVES
To understand confrontation in drama; to understand how life has changed for children since 1948.

CURRICULUM LINKS
History KS2: 2a, 2b, 3, 4b, 11b.
QCA History: Unit 13 – How has life in Britain changed since 1948?

What you need
Safe, open space; whiteboard or flipchart; pens.

What to do
● Divide the board into two sections headed 'Present' and '1948'.
● Ask the children to think of luxuries that they have in their lives and daily chores they have to perform. Luxuries might include mobile phones, personal televisions, computers and getting lifts to school every day; chores might include cleaning up their bedrooms and doing the washing-up.
● Now ask the class to think about life after World War Two and to consider the luxuries that children had and the chores they had to do in 1948. For example, a bag of sweets would have been considered a luxury, and children may have had to walk to school, help to clean the house on a regular basis or help to prepare the dinner.
● Encourage the children to come up to the board and write their examples down.
● Discuss in detail the disadvantages of what being a child was like in 1948. For example, there was no central heating so it was always very cold in winter.
● Invite the children to think about the same question and discuss the disadvantages of what being a child is like in today's society.
● Encourage the children to write their examples on the board.
● Divide the class into pairs: one in each pair will be a child from 1948 and one will be a child from the present.
● Tell the children that you want them to argue who has the better life. Explain that each child has to argue their case by highlighting the positive aspects of their life and picking out the disadvantages of living in the other child's era.
● When you are satisfied that they are on the right track, give them five minutes of rehearsal time.
● When the five minutes is up, invite each pair to perform their scenes to the rest of the class.
● At the end of each performance, invite constructive criticism from the rest of the class.

Differentiation
Help younger children to prepare the questions so the exercise will be easier. Allow for more rehearsal time if needed. For more able children, select other periods between 1948 and the present, and look at the advantages and disadvantages of living at these times, for example, in the 1950s or 1960s.

Drama and
Role-play

AGE RANGE 9–11

LEARNING OBJECTIVES
To learn the importance of characterisation in drama; to consider different aspects of Victorian life.

CURRICULUM LINKS
History KS2: 2b, 6b, 11a, 11b.
QCA History: Unit 11 – What was it like for children living in Victorian Britain?

The time machine

What you need
Safe, open space.

What to do
● Ask the children to sit quietly in a circle.

● When the children are composed, ask them to shut their eyes and to imagine that they are a child who lived in Victorian Britain.

● While their eyes are shut, ask them to answer your questions in their head. Ask them questions such as *What is your name? How old are you? Do you have any brothers or sisters? What do you do during the day? Do you have an accent? Are you hungry? What is your school like?* and so on.

● When all the children have opened their eyes, ask them to share their thoughts and visualisations that they experienced, with the rest of the class.

● Divide the children into three groups. Group 1 is 'Victorian children at school', group 2 is 'Victorian children at home' and group 3 is 'Victorian children at work'.

● Allocate a director for each group and ask them to create a scene about their given situation, which focuses on the different status of each character.

● Remind the children to concentrate on the appropriate rules and regulations of that time, for example, in schools and factories.

● Suggest to each group that they choose a scribe to write down what the scene is about and to note prompts for the group.

● Tell the children that the aim is to gain an insight into what living in Victorian Britain was like for children.

● Walk around the three groups making sure that they are on the right track and giving direction where it is needed.

● When the groups have finished rehearsing, ask them to perform their scenes to the rest of the class.

● Encourage the class to give constructive feedback to each group, focusing on areas in which the scenes could be improved.

● Ask the three groups to take on board the suggestions that have been made and rehearse the scene again.

● When you are satisfied that the groups are fully rehearsed, invite other classes to come and see your children's insight into what living during Victorian Britain was like.

Differentiation
With younger children, you may find that more teacher input and direction will be required.

AGE RANGE 10–11

LEARNING OBJECTIVES
To learn the importance of credibility and 'sticking to your character' in drama; to look at what life was like in Ancient Greece.

CURRICULUM LINKS:
History KS1 and KS2: 5a, 5b, 5c, 12.
QCA History: Unit 14 – Who were the Ancient Greeks?

Guess the liar!

What you need
Safe, open space; whiteboard or flipchart; pens; 'Guess the liar!' photocopiable page 21 (one copy for each member of the class).

What to do:
● Hand out a copy of 'Guess the liar!' to each member of the class.
● Tell them that the object of the activity is to find out which person out of a group is a 'liar', by listening carefully to what they say.
● Start a discussion on life in Ancient Greece. Encourage the children to ask questions to organise their ideas, for example, *What clothes did the Ancient Greeks wear? Which gods did they worship?* and so on. Write down their ideas on the board.
● When you are satisfied that there is enough information, ask the children to shut their eyes. Tell them that you are going to go round the class and pat some of the children on the back.
● Pat approximately a third of the children on the back, making a mental note of their names.
● Ask the children to open their eyes and tell them that they have to do the following task on their own.
● Ask those who were patted on the back to devise a realistic Greek character from the truthful information on the board. Ask those who were not patted on the back to create a character who is pretending to be from Ancient Greece, but is actually not from Ancient Greece. Explain that the characters who are 'lying' should be clever about what they say. They have to try to convince the people listening that they are Ancient Greeks, even though their facts are wrong.
● All the children should write down facts about their character in the speech bubbles on the photocopiable sheet.
● When you are satisfied that all of the group have completed the exercise, call out one of the children who was patted on the back, along with two who were not. In turn, ask the three children to talk in character about themselves to the rest of the group.
● When the speeches are finished, invite the rest of the class to vote on which character they think is from Ancient Greece.
● At the end of the vote, the character from Ancient Greece steps forward and reveals himself or herself.

Differentiation
With younger children, spend more time on the brainstorming section and carefully explain what you are going to do in the task before starting it. Ask more able children to think carefully about the exercise and to choose facts that will make it difficult to guess, for example, describing clothes that are very like those worn by Ancient Greeks, but not quite right.

Drama and Role-play

Please sir!

Drama and
Role-play

Rumour chain

The Great Fire of London

My character: _____

My job: _____

My age: _____

How did the fire affect me? _____

_____

_____

_____

_____

Tell my story

Name:

Age:

Address:

My portrait

Do you have any brothers or sisters?

What is your favourite food?

What is your favourite colour?

Do you have any pets and where do you keep them?

What is school like?

Do you get a lot of homework?

Do you need to wear gas masks to school?

Have you ever seen a bomb? If so, what was it like?

What jobs do you have to do around the house?

When you are not at school, what games do you play?

Drama and Role-play **BRIGHT IDEAS**

Guess the liar!

Geography

AGE RANGE 5–7

LEARNING OBJECTIVES
To look at the importance of language in drama; to find out what your local town has to offer visitors.

CURRICULUM LINKS
Geography KS1: 3a–e, 4a.
QCA Geography: Unit 1 – Around our school/local area.

Holiday town

What you need
Safe, open space.

What to do
● Ask the children to sit quietly in a circle with their hands placed in front of their laps.
● Invite the children to think about the area where they live. Encourage the children to think of places that might be of interest to people visiting the area for the first time. Ask questions such as, *Does our town have a museum? Does it have a good selection of shops? Is there entertainment in the local area for all age groups?* and so on.
● Encourage the children to give evidence with their examples.
● When you are satisfied with their examples, explain to the children that they are going to pretend to work in a tourist office.
● Explain to the children what a tourist office is and give examples of the work it does, so they fully understand it. Ask if they know whether your town has a tourist office or whether any of them have been to one on holiday.
● Divide the class into smaller groups of four or five, allocating a leader to each group.
● Explain that they will be devising a television advertisement to sell their local area to members of the public who have never visited before. The advertisement must cover places of interest and people's experiences of the area.
● Give the groups 15 minutes to devise their advertisements. Inform the leader of each group that they will be directing the advertisement.
● Explain to the groups that their advertisement must be no more than one minute and 30 seconds in length, and that every member of the group should have a part.
● Walk around the groups as they work, checking that they understand what they are doing and that everyone is involved.
● When the groups have finished, invite them one at a time to come to the front of the class and perform their advertisement.
● At the end of each performance, ask the rest of the class to take a vote on whether they would visit the local area after seeing the advertisement.

Differentiation
Make sure that more able children include more material on heritage and culture within the area in their advertisements, or tell them that the advertisement must appeal more to adults than to children. Focus less able children on appealing to their own age group.

AGE RANGE 6–8

LEARNING OBJECTIVES
To speak in front of an audience; to understand how your local area's safety could be improved.

CURRICULUM LINKS
Geography KS1: 1a–c, 5a.
QCA Geography: Unit 2 – How can we make our local area safer?

Freeze and action

What you need
Safe, open space; whiteboard or flipchart; pens; paper; pencils.

What to do
● Ask the class what they think needs to be done in their local area to make it safer.
● Explain to the class that everyone has beliefs that they feel strongly about. Share your own feelings about a local issue where you feel people could act more responsibly, for example, *I don't like the fact that there is always a lot of litter in the park.*
● Clarify why this issue annoys you.
● Encourage the children to think carefully about something that annoys them and that they feel is not supporting the public's interest.
● Write down their ideas on the board.
● After discussion, explain to the children that you would like them to work individually for this exercise.
● Hand out some paper and pencils, and ask the children to write down what they would like changed in their local area and their reasons why.

● Encourage the children to think carefully about the issue and to give as many reasons as they can to support the change.
● Once you are satisfied that they have completed their task, ask the children to shut their eyes.
● Tell the children that you want them to create a character. Once they have created this character, they will be interviewed by a 'news reporter'.
● Ask the children a series of questions, telling them that they must answer in their head. The questions should help them to create their characters, for example, *How old are you? What is your name? What do you do for a living? Do you have an accent? Are you in a good or bad mood?* and so on.
● When you have finished the questions, ask the children to open their eyes.
● Explain to the children that you would now like them to become that character. Divide the children into groups of four and ask one group to stand in front of the rest of the class. Allocate a child from another group to pretend to be a news reporter.
● When you call out *Action*, the news reporter must ask each of the characters how they would like safety in the local area to be improved.
● Repeat this for the other groups. At the end of each group performance, invite constructive criticism from the rest of the class.
● Inform the children that this type of interview is called a 'vox pop'. A vox pop finds out public opinion and public interests by talking to ordinary people in the street.

Differentiation
With less able children, ask more character questions when they are imagining their characters. Let them use the notes they made about changing the local area as prompts, when the news reporter is interviewing them.

Drama and Role-play

AGE RANGE 6–12

LEARNING OBJECTIVES
To learn the importance of listening and storytelling in drama; to look at different cultures.

CURRICULUM LINKS
Geography KS1: 1a, 3a, 3b.
Geography KS2: 1e, 3a, 6b.
QCA Geography: Unit 24 – Passport to the world.

The telephone

What you need
Whiteboard or flipchart; pens; 'My long-distance friend' photocopiable page 32 (one copy for each child); chair; table; telephone.

What to do
● Ask the children to think of examples of telephone calls that they have received or have witnessed, where good or bad news was communicated. Discuss the children's experiences.

● Ask the children if they have any friends who live in another country. Make a note on the whiteboard of the countries that their long-distance friends live in.

● Encourage the children to think of the differences between their own country and that of their long-distance friends. Invite them to think about the climate, schooling and their home conditions. Make further notes on the board of the differences between countries.

● Hand out copies of 'My long-distance friend' and tell the children that you would like them to quietly work on their own to complete the sheet. Children who do not have a real friend living in another country can make up an imaginary long-distance friend using the notes on the board.

● While the children are working, set up the chair, table and telephone at the front of the class.

● Explain to the children that you want them to improvise a performance in which they receive a telephone call from their long-distance friend, delivering some good or bad news.

● Talk about the kind of news that the friend might be communicating and encourage them to think of details that will make the improvisation more realistic. For example, if their friend from India has just had a new baby brother, they will need to think of a suitable name.

● Discuss how they can make the improvisation realistic by remembering to pause and listen. During the pauses, encourage them to 'listen' in their heads to the questions and responses of their friend. They should react to the news that is delivered by using facial expressions to convey their emotions.

● Emphasise the importance of storytelling in this improvisation. The audience should believe that they are having a real conversation.

Differentiation
With less able children, give them more time to work on the photocopiable sheet and make sure that the exercise is clear. They could also work in pairs, to deliver both sides of the conversation. With older children, set a time limit of two minutes for their improvisation, allowing plenty of time for pauses in conversation as good or bad news is delivered.

Drama and
Role-play

AGE RANGE 7–11

LEARNING OBJECTIVES
To look at the use of improvisation in drama; to study what life is like in India.

CURRICULUM LINKS
Geography KS2: 1e, 3b, 3f, 6b.
QCA Geography: Unit 10 – A village in India.

Pen-friends

What you need
Safe, open space; whiteboard or flipchart; pens; paper; pencils.

What to do
● Ask the children to sit quietly.
● When you have their attention, ask the children if any of them have a pen-friend and where their pen-friends live.
● Encourage the children who have them to explain what a pen-friend is to the rest of the group.
● Ask the children to brainstorm words that they associate with India and Indian culture. Include topics such as schooling and family life. Write their ideas on the board.
● When you are satisfied with the brainstorming session, inform the children that they will be working on their own for this exercise.
● Ask the children to shut their eyes and imagine that they have an Indian pen friend. Ask them a series of questions that they must answer in their heads. Your questions could include, *What is your pen-friend's name? How old is he or she? Does your pen-friend go to school? What does he or she study? Does your pen-friend have any brothers or sisters? What has he or she been up to lately? What is your pen-friend's home like?* and so on.
● When the questioning has finished, ask the children to sit in a circle. Hand out paper and pencils, and ask the children to individually brainstorm their ideas about their imaginary pen-friends.
● Explain to the children that you want each of them to open an imaginary letter from their Indian pen-friend and improvise its contents to the rest of the group. The letter can contain good or bad news. The improvisation should be up to 45 seconds long.
● Stress the importance of working out a firm structure for the improvisation, for example, the opening of the letter, the delivery of the news, the ending of the letter and so on.
● Give the class two minutes to prepare the exercise in their heads.
● Invite one child to come to the centre of the circle and perform their improvisation. Make sure that you time it, and when it is finished give feedback, praising content and authenticity.
● Repeat the exercise, making sure each member of the class has a turn.

Differentiation
Encourage more able children to give a more animated performance, to consider mood and atmosphere, and to add interesting content. Less able or shy children will need encouragement on performance and speaking in front of an audience.

 Drama and Role-play

AGE RANGE 8–11

LEARNING OBJECTIVES
To combine activity and speech in drama; to look at other countries and their cultures.

CURRICULUM LINKS
Geography KS2: 1a, 3b, 3f, 3d, 3g, 6b.
QCA Geography: Unit 18 – Connecting ourselves to the world.

Email me!

What you need
Two chairs; two tables.

What to do
● Place the two sets of tables and chairs next to each other.
● Ask the children in the class if they use the Internet and whether they have an email account.
● Encourage the children to give examples of who they usually email and why they email.
● Explain to the children that the Internet is a very powerful tool that can gather information on almost any given subject by pressing just a few buttons. Explain that email is also extremely powerful as it can get a message to someone across the other side of world in a very short time. If two people are online at the same time, they can hold an email conversation.
● Encourage the children to give examples of the different ways in which email can be used. For example, you can send documents and digital images, and members of your family can send each other holiday snaps.
● Ask the children to get into pairs.
● Inform the children that they will be performing a small sketch using the tables and chairs at the front of the class.
● Explain that the sketch is called 'Email me!'. In it, two children sit back-to-back in the chairs (not looking at each other), with the tables in front of them, and pretend to use keyboards to hold an online conversation with each other.
● Ask the children to discuss what their email conversation will be about. Will they play themselves or will they create characters? Who are they and what countries will be involved? If the children are playing characters from different countries, encourage authenticity in their choice of names and places. Some examples of possible scenarios include a supplier and customer, for example, a lady from India sending saris to England, long-distance pen-friends exchanging news and views, a stamp collector trying to get hold of the one stamp they need to complete their collection from someone in China and so on.
● Encourage the children to hold interesting conversations.
● Give the pairs ten minutes of rehearsal time, informing them that the sketch must be no longer than one minute and 30 seconds in length.
● When they have finished rehearsals, invite the pairs to come up and share their improvisation with the rest of the group.
● At the end of each improvisation, encourage constructive criticism from the rest of the group.

Differentiation
Steer more able children away from just having a normal conversation with an email friend. Encourage them to imagine, for example, that they are collectors of something, long-lost friends or a boss and employee. Encourage older children to use more interesting content and to gain greater insight into the power of email in sharing information around the world.

Drama and Role-play

AGE RANGE 6–11

LEARNING OBJECTIVES
To look at storytelling techniques; to understand the effects of severe weather conditions.

CURRICULUM LINKS
Geography KS1: 3a, 4b; KS2: 3a, 3d, 6e.
QCA Geography: Unit 24 – Passport to the world.

Disaster story

What you need
Safe, open space.

What to do
● Ask the children to think of different weather conditions and invite them to share their examples with the rest of the group.

● Explain that some countries suffer from severe weather conditions, for example, the Caribbean and the East Coast of America suffer from high winds known as hurricanes, and parts of Asia have earthquakes.

● Ask the children if they have heard of these severe weather conditions. Can they give examples, explain what a hurricane or an earthquake is, or describe the effects these weather conditions can have?

● Group the children in fours or fives, and allocate a leader to each group.

● Explain that you would like them to deliver a news bulletin from a destination in the world that has just suffered a severe weather disaster.

● The bulletin must include a studio-based news reader, a reporter on location, a family that has been affected by the disaster, and an expert who can talk about the severe weather condition and of what to expect next.

● The bulletin should start with the news reader in the studio, introducing the story. Then, it moves to a reporter interviewing witnesses at the scene of the disaster, and ends with the expert being interviewed back in the studio.

● Encourage the children to think about the different ways they could tell the disaster story.

● Give the children ten minutes of preparation time.

● Walk around the room, making sure that each group understands the task.

● When each group has finished, invite them to perform their bulletins one at a time.

● At the end of each bulletin, invite constructive criticism from the rest of the group.

Differentiation
Encourage more able children to demonstrate more emotion in their work. They should show how this disaster has affected the family concerned. Allow less able children to focus on the format of the bulletin and watch them carefully when it comes to rehearsal. Do not allow them to become side tracked and encourage the children to stick to the brief set. Allow more rehearsal time if necessary.

AGE RANGE 8–11

LEARNING OBJECTIVES
To deliver messages through drama; to understand how the local environment can be improved.

CURRICULUM LINKS
Geography KS2: 1a, 1d, 2g, 3e, 5a, b.
QCA Geography: Unit 8 – Improving the environment; Unit 21 – How can we improve the area we see from our window?

Clean our streets!

What you need
Safe, open space.

What to do
● Ask the children if they know what is being done in their local area to ensure a cleaner, pollution-free environment. Encourage them to give evidence to support their answers.

● Ask them what they would like to see being done to improve their local environment. For example, should there be more dustbins in the local park?

● Invite the children to say what they would do to change matters if they were in charge.

● After discussion, divide the class into groups of four or five, and allocate a leader to each group.

● Ask the groups to devise a 'Government warning' television advertisement on the effects of pollution in our environment and what must be done to stop it.

● The advertisement should have 'before' and 'after' elements to it. The 'before' element should show the environment being neglected and the 'after' element should demonstrate the improvements that have been made. A narrator will talk throughout the advertisement, while the message must be delivered in mime.

● Within their groups, the children should discuss examples of the 'before' and 'after' elements to be contained in their advertisement.

● When you are satisfied with their examples, give the groups ten minutes to devise their advertisements, making sure that the allocated leaders are in charge of the direction of the piece.

● Walk around the groups as they practise, to ensure that they understand the exercise. After ten minutes, ask the children to sit down in a circle

● Invite the groups in turn to perform their advertisements to the rest of the class.

● At the end of each advertisement, open up a discussion for constructive feedback, asking how the group could have improved their performance.

● Make sure that the feedback is delivered in a positive way. The children could vote to say which advertisement they preferred and offer reasons why it was their favourite.

Differentiation
For less able children, allow more preparation time by offering extra rehearsal time. Focus the group's work on a smaller area, such as the school.

Drama and Role-play

AGE RANGE 9–11

LEARNING OBJECTIVES
To learn the importance of stillness and expression in drama; to look at the roles of village settlers in the past.

CURRICULUM LINKS
Geography KS2: 5b, 6d.
QCA Geography: Unit 9 – Village settlers.

Village life

What you need
Safe, open space; whiteboard or flipchart; marker pens.

What to do
● Ask the children if they know what 'live art' or 'sculpture' are. Listen to some of their interpretations, and invite comments and suggestions from others.
● Explain to the children that through stillness, sculpture and live art can demonstrate a message.
● Tell the children that their task today is to create a tableau or living picture that depicts the life of village settlers in the past. Explain that a tableau is a still scene that gives a message.
● Start a discussion about village life in past times. Remind the children that most people lived off the land. Ask them to think of words that they associate with 'village life in the past' to focus their thoughts. Write these words down on the board.
● After discussion, divide the class into groups of five or six, and allocate a leader to each group. The groups should then start to devise their tableaux.
● The tableaux should look at various aspects of village life, for example, vegetable growing, rearing animals in the paddock, collecting chickens eggs, cooking in the kitchen and so on.
● Each member of the group should develop a character. For example, they should choose a name, decide what their relationship is to the rest of the group and decide what they are doing.
● Once the children have developed their characters, ask the leaders to organise their groups to create its tableau.
● The groups should take turns to perform the tableaux to the rest of the group.
● Allow them to hold their positions for one minute. Then ask the children to step out of their positions, one character at a time, and explain who they are in relation to the picture.
● Encourage the rest of the group to ask questions when each character steps out of the tableau.

Differentiation
Encourage more able children to use more expression in the piece. Ask them to concentrate on their characters' histories and the current moods they are in. Groups of more able children can include diverse activities in the scene. Less able children should concentrate on one aspect of village life, for example, working together in the kitchen or in the vegetable garden.

AGE RANGE 10–11

LEARNING OBJECTIVES
To learn the importance of characterisation in drama; to understand the different structures of a river.

CURRICULUM LINKS
Geography KS2: 2a, 2e, 6c, 7c.
QCA Geography: Unit 14 – Investigating rivers.

The scientists

What you need
Safe, open space; whiteboard or flipchart; pens.

What to do
● Invite the children to sit in a circle.
● Ask them if they know what the word 'improvisation' means. (To make up a sketch on the spot, taking into account props or ideas set by the teacher.)
● Encourage the children to support their answers with evidence and examples of improvisations in which they have participated in the past.
● Ask the children to think of words that they associate with a scientist. Concentrate on appearance, speech, physicality and mood.
● Do the children know of any scientists and what their work involves?
● Write their examples on the board.
● Ask the children to think about the different physical features of rivers, such as waterfalls, meanders, lakes and estuaries. Write their examples on the board. Then ask them to pick out half-a-dozen words or phrases that stand out.
● Group the children into pairs. Tell them that they have five minutes to prepare an improvisation to perform in front of the rest of the class.
● The improvisation is a television programme of two scientists explaining and demonstrating different features in rivers. For example, the scientists could explain a diagram showing how a meander is created in a river.
● Give the children five minutes of preparation time to select information and organise the structure of their improvisation.
● Remind the children to concentrate on conveying facts and information in a clear and concise manner.
● When the five minutes are up, invite each pair in turn to come to the front of the classroom and deliver their improvisation.
● At the end of each improvisation, invite constructive criticism from the rest of the class emphasising its positive delivery.

Differentiation
For less able children, concentrate on the characterisation of the scientists. Spend more time on the description of the scientists, for example, how they would talk about rivers and what kind of props they would need to convey the information.

Drama and
Role-play

AGE RANGE 9–11

LEARNING OBJECTIVES
To speak with confidence in front of an audience; to understand how to look after the local environment.

CURRICULUM LINKS
Geography KS2: 1a, 1b, 1c, 1e, 5a, b.
QCA Geography: Unit 12 – Should the High Street be closed to traffic?

Stop pollution!

What you need
'Stop pollution!' photocopiable page 33 (one copy for each child); pens; pencils; whiteboard or flipchart.

What to do
● Explain that pollution is a subject that many people feel strongly about. Share your own thoughts about pollution and ask the children for their views.

● Ask the children why they think pollution is a bad thing and write down their ideas on the board.

● Explain why pollution makes you cross, for example, some children have problems with their breathing when air quality is poor. While you speak, maintain eye contact with the children and use gesture for emphasis.

● Give a copy of 'Stop pollution!' to each child. They should use it to write down their ideas on how to prevent pollution, for example, not allowing cars to use high streets in town centres.

● Encourage the children to use their personal experience as a basis for their examples.

● When they have finished, explain that they are going to present their reasons and suggestions for stopping pollution to the rest of the class.

● Remind them of the techniques for public speaking that you modelled earlier, for example, eye contact and gesture. Ask them to be enthusiastic while speaking, like a politician who is passionate about his or her cause.

● Give them five minutes of preparation time, practising with a partner.

● When they are ready, invite four of the children to come to the front of the class and give their short speeches.

● Encourage other members of the class to ask questions.

● Repeat the process until all the children have had a turn. Invite constructive criticism from the rest of the class after each group of four.

Differentiation
With more able children, introduce heckling. Concentrate on the delivery with less able children, including gesture and eye contact, and discourage questions that challenge their suggestions. It may be easier to focus on one or two examples of pollution and how to prevent or reduce them.

Drama and Role-play

My long-distance friend

What does your friend look like?
(Draw a picture in the box)

What is your friend's name?

_____

_____

Where does your friend live?

_____

_____

How old is your friend?

_____

_____

Does your friend have any brothers or sisters?

_____

_____

What is your friend's school like?

_____

_____

What activities does your friend enjoy?

_____

_____

Does your friend have any pets?

_____

_____

What does your friend want to be when he or she is grown up?

_____

_____

Drama and
Role-play

Stop pollution!

Complete the speech bubbles to show what we can do to stop pollution.

Science

AGE RANGE 5–7

LEARNING OBJECTIVES
To look at the importance of group bonding; to understand that electricity needs a complete circuit to flow.

CURRICULUM LINKS
Science KS1: Sc4 1b, 1c.
QCA Science: Unit 2F – Using electricity.

Current

What you need
Large, open space; two chairs; number of books.

What to do
● Tell the children that they are going to play a game called 'Current', which demonstrates how electricity needs an unbroken circuit in order to work.
● Ask the children what they know about circuits in electricity and how they work.
● Divide the children into two groups and ask each group to sit in a circle.
● Place a chair by each group and put a pile of books on the floor next to the chair. Use the same number of books for each group, unless one group has one more child. In this case, make the game fairer by giving the smaller group an extra book.
● Number the children in each group, for example, the child nearest to the chair is child 1, the child next to him or her, in a clockwise direction is child 2 and so on.
● Child 1 squeezes child 2's hand, then child 2 squeezes child 3's hand, and so on round the circle until the 'current' is passed back to child 1. Then child 1 gets up, grabs a book, runs around the outside of the circle, and places the book on the chair.
● Child 1 sits back down and child 2 restarts the 'current'. Emphasise that they must all be holding hands in order for the current to begin again because that is how circuits work.
● If the circuit is broken, the group will need to begin counting again with whoever started off the circuit.
● The game keeps going until all the books have been moved from the floor on to the chair. The first group to complete the exercise is the winner.
● Ensure that the children are all holding hands in the circle, to stress the importance of an unbroken circuit.

Differentiation
With less able children, clearly state the safety issues and make sure that they thoroughly understand the game before you start. With older and more able children, be aware of the discipline of the game and ensure that they do not become too competitive.

Drama and Role-play

BRIGHT IDEAS

AGE RANGE 7–9

LEARNING OBJECTIVES
To look at the use of mime and mirroring in drama; the importance of cleaning teeth properly.

CURRICULUM LINKS
Science KS2: Sc2 2a.
QCA Science: Unit 3A – Teeth and eating.

Bathroom mirror

What you need
Open space.

What to do
● Divide the group into pairs, labelling the members of each pair 'A' and 'B'.
● Ask the children when they brush their teeth. Why do they brush their teeth at these times of day?
● Do the children know what certain teeth in their mouths are called and what their purposes are during eating? For example, the molars are used to reduce the food into smaller pieces that are easier to swallow.

● Ask the pairs to sit cross-legged in front of each other.
● Child A should pretend that they are looking in the mirror to brush their teeth (using a regular toothbrush rather than an electric one).
● Child B should pretend to be the reflection in the bathroom mirror, and must copy everything that child A does.
● Remind child A to move very slowly so that child B can pick up movements accurately.
● Child A should brush all of their teeth, reaching for the molars at the back. Remind them to think about the proper method of brushing teeth (up and down, rather than side to side).
● When you are satisfied that each pair have mirrored well, ask them to swap roles.
● Once they have done this, repeat the exercise again, this time concentrating on eating. Encourage them to mime eating with imaginary knives and forks, and to demonstrate how food is chewed. Remind them about the functions of different teeth: teeth at the front are used for biting; teeth at the back are used for chewing.
● Emphasise that the mime must be performed slowly to accurately represent mirroring and reflection.
● If you feel some pairs are stronger than the others, ask them to perform their mime to the rest of the group. Compliment them on their pace and accuracy.

Differentiation
Encourage less able children to use exaggerated movements, so that the actions are clear and easier to mirror. Make sure that more able children concentrate on every area of their face. Encourage the mime to be slow so that it becomes difficult for the person watching to guess which child is the mirror.

Drama and Role-play

AGE RANGE 7–9

LEARNING OBJECTIVES
To use role-play; to think about the different habitats in which animals live and what living creatures need to survive.

CURRICULUM LINKS
Science KS2: Sc2 1a, 1c, 5b.
QCA Science: Unit 4 – Habitats.

My habitat

What you need
Safe, open space; whiteboard or flipchart; pens.

What you do
● Divide the children into groups of three or four.
● Tell them that they will be investigating habitats. Do they know what a habitat is? A habitat is the natural place and environment where animals and plants live.
● Ask them for examples of habitats, such as a field, pond, hedge or tree. Write their suggestions on the board.
● Now ask the children to give an example of living creatures that can be found in each of their suggested habitats.
● Tell the children that they will be acting out a short sketch to look at how animals live in particular habitats.
● Give each group a habitat and ask them to think about the different types of creatures that live there.
● Encourage the children to think about how the creatures survive in this habitat. Where do they live and sleep? What do they eat? How do they find their food?
● Each group should pick an animal and devise a sketch to show how that animal lives in their group's habitat. They can either use mime or describe their habitat as they perform, for example, *I live high up in a tree and I build my home with lots of twigs. I like to eat worms but it is not easy trying to find them from the air. (I'm a bird.)*
● Allow ten minutes for the groups to discuss and practise the sketches. Then invite each group in turn to perform its sketch. The rest of the class have to guess what animal the members of the group are role-playing.

Differentiation
For less able children, keep the focus on the local environment or a specific location, for example, *What kind of animals can be found in a field?* Older and more able children can work in groups to look at different animals that live in the same kind of habitat, or to investigate food chains.

Drama and Role-play

BRIGHT IDEAS

Argument cycle

AGE RANGE 7–11

LEARNING OBJECTIVES
To look at the use of argument in drama; to look at the nature of life cycles.

CURRICULUM LINKS
Science KS2: Sc2 2f.
QCA Science: Unit 5b – Life cycles.

What you need
'Argument cycle' photocopiable page 42 (enlarged to A3-size or one copy for each group).

What to do
● Discuss the picture on the 'Argument cycle' photocopiable sheet. The mother is telling her daughter off for making a mess and the grandmother is telling the mother off for being too strict with the daughter.

● Explain that each character is at a different stage of the life cycle. Ask the children to think about different phases in the life cycle: child, teenager, adult, parent and grandparent. What are people like at these different stages? What roles do they play? What might their concerns be?

● Seat the children in a circle. Pick three volunteers to stand in the centre.

● Label the volunteers, 'Grandparent', 'Parent' and 'Child'.

● Ask the grandparent to start an argument with the parent, for example, the mother is too strict with her daughter or the father has not fixed his car.

● When that argument finishes, the parent turns to the child and starts another argument, for example, the child never cleans their bedroom or they never eat the food that is cooked for them.

● When that argument finishes, the child turns to the grandparent and starts another argument, for example, the television is too loud or they do not like the dinner that the grandparent has cooked.

● The conflicts should reflect the concerns of people at different stages in life and should end with positive resolutions.

● Vary the activity with alternative scenarios, for example, a parent and two siblings of very different ages. The argument could be about the older child having to look after the younger one.

● Repeat the exercise with different groups of three children.

Differentiation
For less able children, make sure that they understand the cycle of the exercise rather than the arguments. Spend some more time on discussing the life cycle and what people's concerns are at the different stages of life, so that the children can empathise more with their character. With more able children, encourage a more in-depth exercise, focusing on each argument and allowing the sketches to run for longer.

AGE RANGE 8–10

LEARNING OBJECTIVES
To look at emotional and physical states in drama; to think about how climate and our surroundings can affect us.

CURRICULUM LINKS
Science KS2: SC3 2c, 2e.
QCA Science: Unit 4c – Keeping warm.

Hot and cold

What you need
Safe, open space; whiteboard or flipchart; pens.

What to do
● Seat the children in a circle.
● Ask them to shut their eyes and imagine that they are on a beach. The sun is beating down, their bodies feel warm and they can hear the sea lapping around their feet.
● Then ask them to imagine that they are on top of a very high mountain in the middle of snow, ice and wind. They feel very cold.
● Ask the children to open their eyes. Discuss how they felt in each situation, for example, *I felt really cold and uncomfortable, and my feet felt like blocks of ice.* Invite them to explain their emotions, do they feel moody when it's cold and happy when it's warm?
● Group the children in pairs and ask them to label themselves 'A' and 'B'.
● Tell them to plan a sketch in which child A is someone who is cold and child B is someone who is warm. Think of a few ideas together, for example, a child in a swimming pool being watched by a teacher on the side of the pool, someone answering the door to a friend on a cold winter's night, a homeless person and a businessman meeting on the street.
● Ask them to write down the emotional and physical states that go with each character. For example, the cold character might feel cross, sad or stiff while the warm character might feel confident and comfortable.
● Give the pairs ten minutes to work out a sketch.
● Walk around the room, making sure children are on the right track
● Invite the pairs to the front of the class to perform their sketches.
● Explain that, just as a thermometer tells us the temperature, you want the class to guess the temperature in the performed sketches. Use a scale on the board to say whether the temperature is 'very hot', 'hot', 'warm', 'cool', 'cold' or 'very cold'.

Differentiation
With less able children, concentrate on the physical and emotional state of this exercise and less on the characterisation. When their eyes are shut, go into more detail with the images of the beach and the mountain.

Drama and Role-play **BRIGHT IDEAS**

AGE RANGE 9–11

LEARNING OBJECTIVES
To demonstrate dialogue between two characters, concentrating on friction; to think about the rules for healthy living.

CURRICULUM LINKS
Science KS2: Sc1 1a; Sc2 2b, 2d, 2g, 2h.
QCA Science: Unit 5a – Keeping healthy.

You know the rules

What you need
'You know the rules' photocopiable page 43 (one copy for each pair); safe, open space.

What to do
● Ask the children to look at the four cartoons on the 'You know the rules' photocopiable sheet, and to explain what they see. What is the theme of the sheet? (Each cartoon has a health issue involved.)
● Ask them to identify the health issue and to work out what the rule should be for each cartoon. For example, *You must keep your room clean or else you will pick up an infection.*
● Group the children into pairs and ask them to label themselves 'A' and 'B'.
● Explain that they will have five minutes to prepare an improvisation of a scene based on one of the cartoons. Child A will play a character in the cartoon, child B will play a parent or visitor to the scene.
● The improvisation must contain an argument or element of friction, which is then resolved.
● Encourage the pairs to ensure that their improvisations have a beginning, middle and end, and that the audience learns something about keeping healthy.
● Walk around the room observing, checking that each pair is on the right track. Assist them with the scenario if you feel they need guidance.
● When you are satisfied that each pair has finished, invite them to the front of the class to perform their improvisation.
● At the end of each improvisation, invite constructive criticism from the rest of the group.
● Make sure that each health issue is covered and discuss what can be done to improve or help the characters in the cartoons.

Differentiation
With less able children, allow more rehearsal time and give them extra guidance concerning the health issue in each cartoon and the consequences of not dealing with the issues. More able children can think of other scenarios that deal with health issues.

AGE RANGE 9–11

LEARNING OBJECTIVES
To look at the technique of conversation and interview in drama; to think about health issues.

CURRICULUM LINKS
Science KS2: SC2 2b, c, d, g, h.
QCA Science: Unit 5A – Keeping healthy.

Doctor's surgery

What you need
Safe, open space; two chairs; copies of 'The waiting room' photocopiable page 44.

What to do
● Seat the children in a large circle. Hand out copies of 'The waiting room' photocopiable sheet and talk about the picture. What are the people waiting for? Why might they want to talk to the doctor? Discuss the posters on the walls and the health issues they raise.

● Ask if any of the children have been to a doctor's surgery before. Discuss their experiences.

● Explain that people generally go to the surgery for advice from a doctor when they are ill, or when something does not feel right.

● Ask the children to think about how doctors might deal with different ailments and health issues.

● Tell the children that people can go to the doctor for a medical check-up, at which the doctor will ask questions about things that affect a person's health, such as how much they exercise, their diet and if they smoke.

● Ask the children to get into pairs, labelling themselves 'A' and 'B'. Child A is to play the doctor and child B is to play the patient.

● Explain that they have five minutes to work on an improvisation. Child B comes to the surgery suffering certain symptoms, which they must demonstrate, and must explain to child A that they have a health issue that they would like to discuss.

● Encourage the children to use some of the health issues that they have discussed in class. Remind the children about health issues such as smoking, lack of exercise and too much salt and fat in food.

● Walk around the class, making sure that each pair is on the right track.

● When you are satisfied that they have had enough time, invite the pairs to come to the centre of the circle and share their improvisations.

● At the end of each improvisation, encourage constructive criticism by asking the rest of the group if child A (the doctor) missed anything out and if there was anything they would have added.

● When all the pairs are finished, invite them to look at the improvisation again, working on the areas where things were missed out.

Differentiation
With more able children, encourage further character improvisation, for example, a character might have a husky voice because he or she smokes.

Drama and
Role-play

BRIGHT IDEAS

AGE RANGE 9–11

LEARNING OBJECTIVES
To look at the use of the body in drama; to understand the function of joints in movement.

CURRICULUM LINKS:
Science KS2: SC2 2e, f.
QCA Science: Unit 4a – Moving and growing.

Body mirror

What you need
Safe, open space.

What to do
● Group the children into pairs, labelling themselves 'A' and 'B'.
● Ask the children to take a good look at their bodies and see what happens when they move certain parts. For example, *When I wave my hands, my forearms move at the elbow*.
● Ask them if they know what certain joints and bones are called, and what function they have. Explain that joints are important because they allow our skeletons to move. For example, shoulder joints allow us to move our arms.
● Ask the children for other examples of what their joints allow them to do.
● Once you are satisfied with their answers, ask the pairs to sit in front of each other.
● Child A pretends that they are looking in their bedroom mirror and that their body is moving very slowly.
● Child B plays child A's reflection in the bedroom mirror and must copy everything that child A does.
● Remind child A to move very slowly, so that child B can pick up their movements accurately.
● Explain to child A that you would like them to sculpt their body into different shapes. Encourage them to think about the different joints in their body and how they move. When you are satisfied that each pair have mirrored well, ask them to swap roles.
● Then repeat the exercise, this time concentrating on everyday movements, for example, putting on a pair of socks or bending down to empty a bin. Encourage the children to explore their bodies.
● Emphasise to the class that the mime must be performed slowly so that the mirroring and reflection are accurate.
● If you feel a few of the pairs are stronger than the others, ask them to perform their mimes to the rest of the group. Compliment them on their pace and accuracy.
● Ask the rest of the group if they can identify which joints are being used and how they are being used. For example, joints in the hips and knees are used for bending down.

Differentiation
With less able children, concentrate on the slowness of the exercise, making sure that they maintain eye contact with their partner. Simplify the exercise by focusing on individual movements rather than combined actions.

Argument cycle

You know the rules

The waiting room

Drama and
Role-play

CHAPTER 4

Art and design

AGE RANGE 5–7

LEARNING OBJECTIVES
To learn the importance of body language in drama; to study what we look like.

CURRICULUM LINKS
Art and design KS1: 1a, 2c, 5a.
QCA Art and Design: Unit 1a – Self portrait.

Look at me

What you need
Safe, open space.

What to do
● Ask the children to sit in a circle.
● Explain that everyone in the world is different and that we all have our own unique ways of walking and moving. Everyone also has their own way of doing things, whether it be running in a race, dancing to music or standing in a queue.
● Ask for a volunteer to stand in the middle of the circle and perform an action that they do every day and are familiar with, for example, putting a hair bobble in or zipping up a coat.
● Encourage the other members of the class to study the volunteer's action closely.
● Ask for another two volunteers to copy the first volunteer's action, concentrating particularly on facial expression.
● When they are finished, ask the volunteers to go back to their places.
● Invite the children to stand up in the circle.
● Explain that you would like them, individually, to take a step into the circle, to say their name and to strike a pose at the same time. The pose must reflect something of their personality, for example, putting hands on hips or blowing a kiss. The individual then steps back into the circle and the rest of the group step forward and mimic the pose.
● Everyone in the group should take a turn, moving in a clockwise direction around the circle. Each child steps forward and strikes a pose that represents them, and the rest of the group follow with an imitation of the pose.
● You can take the exercise one step further by encouraging the children to demonstrate more movements that they believe represent them.

Differentiation
With more able children, introduce expression and mood. Ask the class to share what they think the mood of the individual is like, based on the pose. The exercise could be developed further to introduce dance.

AGE RANGE 5–7

LEARNING OBJECTIVES
To look at sculpture; to learn the importance of shape, stillness and expression in drama.

CURRICULUM LINKS
Art and design KS1: 4b, 5a.
QCA Art and design: Unit 1c – What is sculpture?

The kitchen

What you need
Safe, open space; kettle; iron; teapot.

What to do
● Ask the children to sit in a large circle. Place the kettle, iron and teapot in the middle.
● Invite the children to verbally describe the shape of each object. For example, *The teapot has a round handle for holding and a long spout for the tea to come out.*
● Encourage the children to pick up the objects and study their shape, size and dimensions.
● Divide the class into groups of six or seven, and allocate a leader to each group.
● Explain that the groups are going to sculpt one of those three kitchen objects using their bodies. Encourage the children to think about the shape and dimensions of the kitchen object when they create their sculpture.
● Give the groups five minutes of preparation time.
● Walk around the room, making sure that the children are on the right track and that they have understood the exercise.
● When the five minutes are up, sit the children back in the circle. Invite one of the groups to come to the centre of the circle to show their sculpture. Ask the remaining children to study the sculpture and to describe what they see. For example, *I can tell that Michelle is the spout by the way she is holding her hands.*
● Repeat the process with all the remaining groups.
● When the groups are finished, extend the sculpture exercise by looking at objects around the room or encourage the children to think of other shapes.

Differentiation
With less able children, concentrate on household objects, focusing on size, shape and dimension. With more able children you can introduce actual sculptures, for example, the work of Henry Moore. Encourage them to think about the message a particular sculpture is trying to convey. Suggest words to help them describe this message, for example, 'happiness', 'jealousy', 'love' and 'hate'.

Drama and
Role-play

AGE RANGE 6–7

LEARNING OBJECTIVES
To study our faces; to make use of our faces in drama.

CURRICULUM LINKS:
Art and design KS1 and KS2: 1a, 4a, 5a.
QCA Art and design: Unit 2B – Mother Nature, designer.

Feeling blue

What you need
'Feeling blue' photocopiable page 55 (one copy for each child), colouring pens, paper.

What to do
● Invite the children to sit in a circle.
● Ask the children what the expression 'feeling blue' means (feeling sad or feeling unhappy). Tell them that colours are often associated with different feelings, for example, red and anger. Can they think of any other examples? (Yellow is often associated with happiness, green is often associated with jealousy and so on.)
● Say that our faces often express our emotional feelings. For example, we smile when we are happy, we cry when we are sad.
● Ask the children to think of different emotional feelings and encourage them to use their faces to give examples.
● Hand out a copy of the 'Feeling blue' photocopiable sheet to each child.
● The sheet shows six different faces, demonstrating six different emotional feelings (anger, happiness, sadness, jealousy, evil and excitement). Ask the children if they know what the feelings are and the reasons why they have made that choice, for example, *I think that man is sad because he is crying.*
● Ask the children to colour each face to demonstrate its mood, for example, a red angry face, a yellow happy face and so on.
● Walk around the circle, making sure that the children are on the right track.
● When they have finished, ask them to stand in a circle.
● Explain that you are going to shout out different colours, for example, red, pink or green. You will then give a five second countdown before shouting out *Freeze!*, and the children must demonstrate that colour with their faces and bodies. For example, if you shouted *Red!,* you would expect the children to look really angry, and their bodies and faces to look aggressive.
● If there are four or five children who are particularly good at this exercise, ask the rest if the group to sit down while you repeat the exercise with the chosen children.

Differentiation
Extend the activity with pairs of more able children. Ask them to choose a colour each, and create a character of that 'colour' (for example, an angry 'red' character, and a crying 'blue' character). They should then make up a scene based on these two characters, for example, a 'red' character scowling at 'blue' character, who is crying because he or she has done something wrong.

AGE RANGE 7–9

LEARNING OBJECTIVES
To investigate pattern; to learn the importance of rhythm and movement in drama.

CURRICULUM LINKS
Art and design KS2: 4a, 5a.
QCA Art and design: Unit 3b – Investigating pattern.

Walk the circle

What you need
Safe, open space.

What to do
● Stand in a circle with the rest of the group.
● Explain that the exercises they will be doing are about investigating pattern.
● Explain that you going to start a pattern, which will then move in an anticlockwise direction around the circle.
● Start with an easy pattern, for example, clapping your hands. The children then take turns copying your action, moving the clapping around the circle until the action gets back to you. Move on to a more difficult pattern that involves using all of your body.
● Explain to the children that a 'pattern' is something (like an action or a design) that is repeated many times – just like what happened in the circle.
● Ask for a volunteer to stand up and walk around the circle, as if they were walking to school. Explain that walking is a pattern, because the same movements are repeated many times.
● Encourage other members of the class to study the volunteer's walk, noting how they hold their heads, swing their arms and where their eyes are facing.
● Ask for a further two volunteers to stand up and start walking around the circle behind the first volunteer. Ask them to mimic his or her walk and concentrate on the rhythm, pace and speed. It will take a while for the children to pick up the momentum of the walk.
● When you feel that they have picked up the pattern of the walk, let them practise it for a while.
● Repeat this exercise with other members of the group, adding more people if required.

Differentiation
Less able children should concentrate on copying a regular walk. With more able children, ask more than a couple of volunteers to follow the leader around the circle, and introduce more complex patterns of movement into the walk, for example, swinging arms in a circular motion, lifting knees up and so on.

Drama and Role-play

AGE RANGE 8–9

LEARNING OBJECTIVE
To learn the importance in drama of themes, and conveying messages through stillness; to think about how pictures can convey a message.

CURRICULUM LINKS
Art and design KS1 and KS2: 1a, 1b, 2c, 5a.
QCA Art and design: Unit 4A – Viewpoints;
Unit 4C – Journeys.

Icarus

What you need
Safe, open space; copies of 'Icarus' photocopiable page 56.

What to do
● Hand out enough copies of the 'Icarus' photocopiable sheet so that all the children can see it comfortably.
● Explain that it shows a Greek myth about a father and son called Daedalus and Icarus.
● Ask a child to read out the brief story of Icarus.
● Explain that the pictures show conflict between two people.
● Discuss with the group what is happening in each picture. Ask for some of the children's interpretations, and invite comments and suggestions from others.
● Ask the children if the pictures or story are trying to give a message. If so, what is the message? What is the theme of the story? (What is it about?) Explain that there may be different messages conveyed in a story, for example, one of the themes in 'Icarus' is the importance of listening to advice; another is the danger of not realising your own limitations.
● Ask the children to support their opinions with evidence from the story, for example, Daedalus' unheeded warning, and the pictures, for example, the characters' facial expressions, stances and positions.
● After the discussion, divide the children into groups of eight.
● Each group is to tell the story of 'Icarus' in the form of four tableaux. Explain that a tableau is a silent and still group of people arranged to show a scene.
● Ask the students to make sure that tableau 1 shows the beginning of the story and tableau 4 the end. These are the most important tableaux when it comes to the group's storytelling.
● Each child should adapt a role from the pictures. Encourage the children to use facial expression, body language and gesture as part of their role-playing.
● When the children have had time to practise, watch some of the tableaux. Ask the rest of the class to offer their opinions on whether the messages in the story came across.
● When the children have finished their tableaux, invite them to create their own story with a similar theme to 'Icarus'. Each tableau should emphasise an important message that the group wants to convey.
● Finally, watch some of the new tableaux all the way through, inviting constructive comments from the rest of the class.

Differentiation
Less able children could use simple short stories with strong narratives and clear messages, such as Aesop's fables. Challenge more able children to experiment with themes that are relevant to their lives.

AGE RANGE 8–11

LEARNING OBJECTIVES
To look at different ways of telling stories in art and drama; to see how different styles of storytelling can affect the mood and atmosphere of a story or piece of art.

CURRICULUM LINKS
Art and design KS2: 5d.
QCA Art and design: Unit 4a – Viewpoints.

Strange tales

What you need
Copies of 'Cinderella' photocopiable page 57; safe, open space; whiteboard or flipchart; pens.

What to do
● Describe a dream that you have had to the children. The dream should be of an everyday scene, but the scene felt disturbing because of the mood or atmosphere.
● Explain that changing the mood or atmosphere of a scene can evoke a completely different response to a story or picture. The style of telling a story, or depicting a scene, has an effect on the person listening to a story or looking at a picture.
● Give out copies of the 'Cinderella' photocopiable sheet. The four pictures show the same scene but the mood and atmosphere in each are different.
● Explain that each picture is in a different 'style': the first picture, for example, is comedy, because funny things are happening and the mood is humorous; the second picture is sad and serious, and is therefore closer to tragedy.
● Ask the children to look at each picture and suggest what style it is in. Encourage them to think of the features that contribute to the different styles. In other words, how can they tell a scene is comic, tragic or scary?
● Encourage the children to use evidence from the pictures to back up their suggestions, for example, *The mice are pushing the flour over the ugly sisters and that's funny, so I think it is a comedy.*
● Divide the children into groups of four.
● Explain that you would like each group to devise a two-minute sketch using one of the scenes on the sheet as a starting point. Allocate a picture to each group.
● Before they start, encourage the children to discuss the style of their picture and to work out how they are going to demonstrate it.
● Emphasise to the children that using a narrator, especially to open and close the scene, might help to tell the story and create mood and atmosphere.
● Give them ten minutes of preparation time. When they are ready, invite the groups to come to the front of the class to present their sketch.

Differentiation
With less able children, spend more time discussing the different styles of the pictures and how this could be conveyed dramatically. Encourage more able children to explore ways of conveying mood and atmosphere more deeply. Allow them more preparation and performance time.

Drama and
Role-play

AGE RANGE 8–11

LEARNING OBJECTIVES
To look at the use of shape in drama; to explore how containers can be made using the body.

CURRICULUM LINKS
Art and design KS1 and KS2: 1a, 5a, 5b, 5c.
QCA Art and design: Unit 5b – Containers.

The submarine

What you need
Safe, open space.

What to do
● Seat the children in a circle.
● Ask them to think of the word 'container'. Encourage the children to explain what the word means and a container's purpose. For example, *A container is an object used to hold, carry or transport things.*
● Explain to the children that there are different types of container. For example, a container that can hold paintbrushes and pens, or a container that can hold people.
● Encourage the children to think of containers that hold

people, for example, aeroplanes, ships and submarines.
● Divide the class into groups of eight, allocating a director to each group.
● Explain that, using their bodies, you would like each group to create a submarine.
● Encourage the children to think of the shape of the submarine and what special features it has, for example, a look-out station and propeller jets.
● Give the groups four or five minutes of preparation time.
● Invite the groups to share their work with the rest of the class.
● Explain to the children that you would now like them to create a scene that takes place inside a submarine, involving a disaster that the crew has to sort out. Ask them to think of what kind of people would be inside the submarine, for example, captains, officers or sailors, and what kind of disaster could take place, for example, colliding with another submarine.
● Explain to the children that they will be stepping inside one of the other groups' submarines that they have made using their bodies, and playing the scene from there.
● Allow five minutes of preparation time.
● Invite the first group to get into the position of the submarine that they have created and the second group to play their scene.

Differentiation
With less able children, just concentrate on building the container. You do not have to use a submarine as your example – any other form of container (or transport that 'contains' people) will do. More able children can develop the idea further by thinking about containers that hold inanimate objects. For example, they could be pencils in a pencil case, jostling for a writer's attention, with the writer opening the container at intervals to pick a pencil.

The museum

AGE RANGE 8–11

LEARNING OBJECTIVES
To look at how museums and galleries deliver messages through themed exhibitions; to explore the use of the body and facial expression to convey a message.

CURRICULUM LINKS
Art and design KS2: 4c, 5c, 5d.
QCA Art and design: Unit 9g – Visiting a museum, gallery or site.

What you need
Safe, open space; book or photographs showing art or sculpture.

What to do
● Ask the children to sit in a circle.

● Explain that a museum or gallery shares historical information or a message with its audience. Sometimes they hold exhibitions or have collections that are based on a theme or that have a message, for example, a theme about recycling to show how we can use re-use objects in different ways.

● Ask the children if they have ever been to a gallery or museum before, and to explain what they saw there and what it was about.

● Encourage the children to give examples of what was in the museum or gallery, and whether they liked it.

● Place a few pictures showing examples of art and sculpture, some of which the children may recognise, in the centre of the circle.

● Invite the children to look at the pictures carefully. Can they see a message or understand what the object or piece of art is trying to tell them? For example, *I can see that those two people in the sculpture are hugging each other, so maybe the message is that they are in love.*

● Divide the class into groups of five or six.

● Explain that each group is to create a piece of still, live art or sculpture that demonstrates a message. They can only use themselves, no props are allowed.

● Encourage the children to work out what their message will be before they start devising.

● Give them three minutes of preparation time, making sure that they have understood what has been set.

● Invite the first group to demonstrate their piece, and ask the other children if they can guess what the message is. Invite constructive criticism from the rest of the class.

● Repeat this for the other groups.

Differentiation
Less able children can use one of the pictures that you put on display as a model, rather than create their own live art. With more able children, allow more preparation time.

Drama and
Role-play

AGE RANGE 9–11

LEARNING OBJECTIVES
To learn the importance of stillness and expression in drama; to consider stories behind photographs.

CURRICULUM LINKS
Art and design KS2: 2c, 3a, 3b.
QCA Art and design: Unit 5a – Objects and meanings.

The photo album

What you need
Safe, open space, collection of different photographs (the locations can vary but they must all include people).

What to do
● Ask the children to sit in a circle.
● Place the collection of photographs in the centre of the circle.
● Invite the children to choose a photograph and study it. Encourage them to look at the faces of the people in the photographs and the surroundings they are in.
● Explain to the children that every photograph tells a story and can also depict a mood. For example, photographs can show if people are fed up or really happy.
● Encourage the children to tell stories about their photographs. Ask them to give evidence for their stories from the photograph, for example, *I think that she is really happy because she has just got the birthday present that she has been waiting for.*
● Divide the class into groups of six, allocating a director for each group.
● Explain that you would like each group to pick one photograph from the collection. They should then recreate the photograph they have chosen. Everyone in the group must be allocated a part in the photograph. The director should then place the rest of the group in position before he or she enters the photograph.
● Tell the children that they must have exactly the same facial expression as the person they are studying in the photograph.
● Wait until the groups have worked out their expressions and positioning. Then tell them that, individually, they must step out of the photograph and give one sentence about how they are feeling, for example, *I am really happy because I have just received the bike I have wanted for ages.*
● When all of the groups have finished practising, invite them to perform in turn.

Differentiation
Less able children should concentrate on mood and expression. Encourage more able children to give their character a name and to explain how they feel about certain people in the photograph when they step out.

AGE RANGE 9–11

LEARNING OBJECTIVES
To learn the importance of props in relation to characterisation and performance; to understand how a person's appearance can convey certain messages.

CURRICULUM LINKS
Art and design KS2: 5a.
QCA Art and design: Unit 6b – What a performance.

The bag of hats

What you need
'The bag of hats' photocopiable page 58 (one copy for each child); collection of different hats; safe, open space.

What to do
● Ask the children to sit in a circle.
● Give one copy of 'The bag of hats' photocopiable sheet to each child.
● Explain that there are eight different hats on the sheet and underneath the hats the children must write down what kind of person they think might wear this hat.
● Help the children to identify the type of hats they are before they start the work.
● Encourage them to give two to three examples for each hat. For example, a woolly hat might be worn by a child going to school or a hiker.

● Place a collection of hats in the centre of the circle.
● Ask the children to identify the hats and encourage them to give examples of people they think might wear them.
● Invite two volunteers to pick a hat each and put it on.
● Ask the rest of the class what kind of characters the volunteers could be. For example, a child wearing the woolly hat could be a hiker and a child wearing a flat cap could be an old man.
● Ask what kind of conversations could take place between these two characters. For example, the old man could be asking the hiker where his favourite places are to walk and where he will be going next.
● Ask the volunteers to make a decision as to what their conversation will be and give them two minutes preparation time. While this is going on, ask for another two volunteers and repeat the process.
● Carry on like this, making time at intervals for pairs to share their sketches with the rest of the class. Once they have done so, they can return their hats to the centre of the circle, to allow another pair to use them.

Differentiation
Allow less able children more discussion of what type of people would wear these hats. Give more preparation time where needed.

Drama and
Role-play

Feeling blue

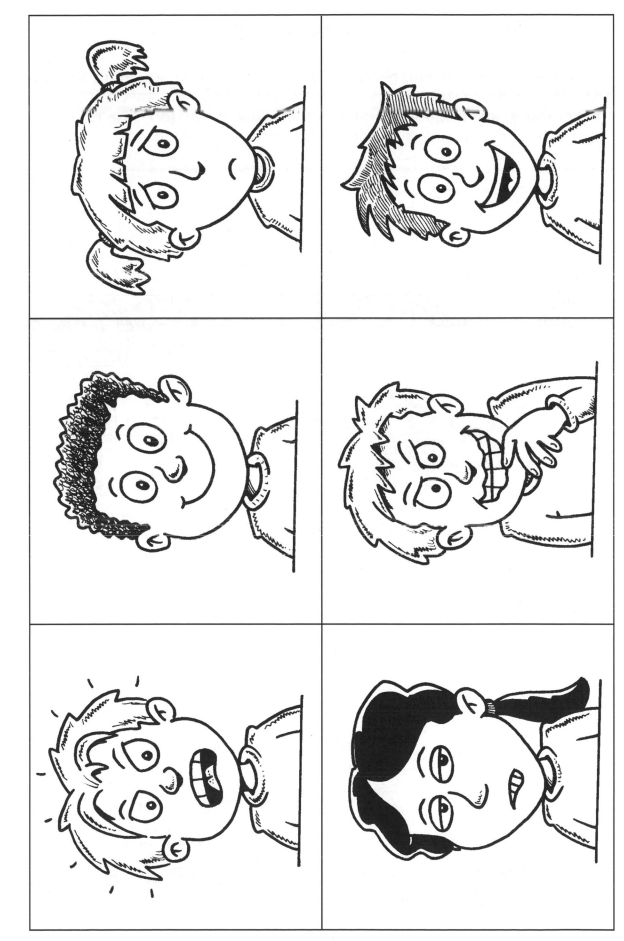

Icarus

Icarus was imprisoned with his father Daedalus in a maze, which his father had built. They escaped by making wings from feathers held together by wax. Overjoyed at the thrill of flying, Icarus ignored his father's advice and flew too close to the sun. The wax melted because it was so hot and Icarus fell to his death.

Drama and Role-play

Cinderella

The bag of hats

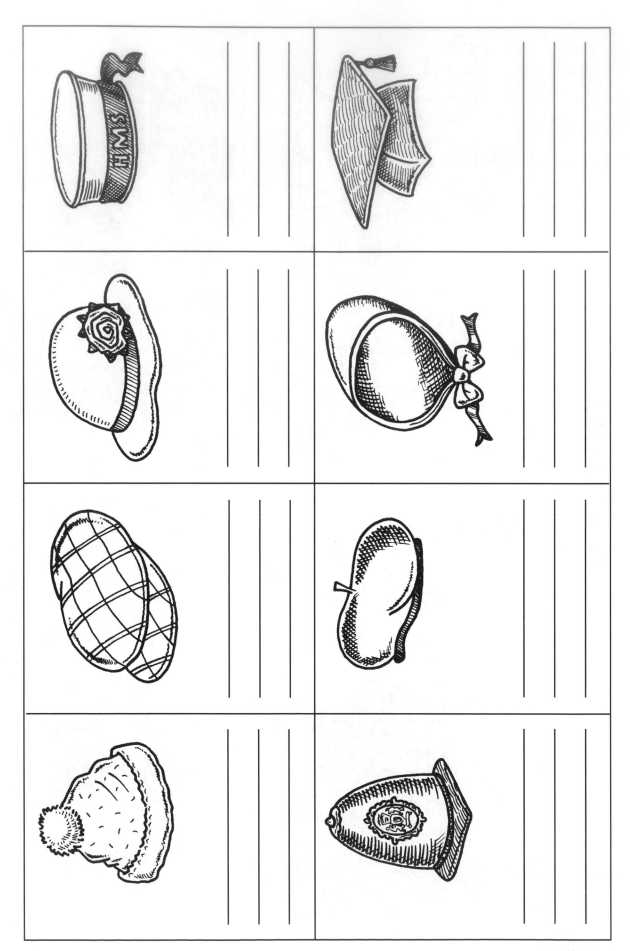

CHAPTER 5

Music

AGE RANGE 5–7

LEARNING OBJECTIVES
To look at the use of sound and expression in drama; to explore different everyday sounds.

CURRICULUM LINKS
Music KS1: 2b, 4a.
QCA Music: Unit 2 – Sounds interesting, Exploring sounds.

The sound circle

What you need
Safe, open space.

What to do
● Ask the children to sit in a large circle.
● Explain that we are surrounded every day by different sounds.
● Encourage the children to think of different sounds that they come across during the day, for example, the car door slamming, the sound of butter being spread on fresh toast and so on.
● Demonstrate a couple of sounds to the children. For example, make a dripping tap sound by closing your mouth and popping your finger out.

● Allow the children a minute to explore making different sounds. They can use their hands, feet, mouth, lips, teeth or voice.
● Ask the children to think of a facial expression or movement of the body that goes with the noises you have suggested. For example, the slamming of the car door might make you jump, the spreading of butter on fresh toast might make you grit your teeth.
● Encourage each child to think of a sound they hear in their home, for example, teeth being brushed, the kettle boiling, the doorbell ringing and so on.
● When everyone has thought of a sound, say that you are going to move around the circle and ask each of them to demonstrate their sound.
● At the end of each sound, the rest of the class has three guesses as to what the sound might be.
● When each child has had a turn, tell them you will now go round the circle again and that this time they must add an expression or body movement that goes with their sound, for example, clenching the body while making the whistling sound of a kettle.
● Give the children one minute of preparation time for this.
● Move around the circle and ask each child in turn to demonstrate their sound with their movement or expression.

Differentiation
Keep the environments simple for less able children as this will help them to make identifiable sounds. Encourage more able children to think of more interesting environments for discovering sounds, for example, modes of transport and restaurants.

AGE RANGE 5–7

LEARNING OBJECTIVES
To explore rhythm and pulse; to experience performing.

CURRICULUM LINKS
Music KS1: 2a, 2b, 5a.
QCA Music: Unit 4 – Exploring pulse and rhythm.

The rhythm circle

Create the beat + band of the songs

What you need
Safe, open space.

What to do
● Ask the children to sit in a large circle.
● Explain that we are surrounded every day by different noises and rhythms.
● Encourage the children to think of different rhythms that they come across during the day, for example, the rhythm of the windscreen wipers on a car, the tick of a clock, the beat of a drum and so on.
● Demonstrate a couple of these rhythms to the children.
● Walk around the circle and ask each child in turn to demonstrate a rhythm, and a movement that goes with it.
● Explain to the children that you would now like them to make a piece of music that involves everyone sharing their rhythms.
● Pick a child who has an easy rhythm, and ask them to demonstrate their rhythm and to repeat it over and over again. This rhythm will start the piece of music.
● Now move around the circle inviting each child in turn to introduce his or her rhythm, making sure that it fits in time with the original rhythm. Make sure that every child's rhythm is involved.
● You may find it helpful to clap in time to the first rhythm to keep a steady beat (or pulse).
● When you are satisfied that the children's music is on the right track, ask them to pause. Explain that you are going to conduct the level of volume of their music. You will do this by raising your arms above your head to indicate increase in volume, and lowering them to indicate decrease in volume.
● Start the music again. Allow a couple of minutes for the children to prepare, then start raising and lowering your arms to change the volume.

Differentiation
If the class is large, divide it into two and allow one group to observe the other. By doing this, the exercise will become more structured and you are less likely to lose the rhythm. With more able children, make sure that you emphasise the importance of sticking to the original rhythm.

Drama and Role-play

AGE RANGE 6-8

LEARNING OBJECTIVES
To explore pitch and melodic patterns; to look at the use of pitch and melodic patterns in dramatic representation.

CURRICULUM LINKS
Music KS1 and KS2: 1a, 3a.
QCA Music: Unit 5 – Taking off, Exploring pitch.

Fantasy battles

What you need
Safe, open space; piece of dramatic instrumental music, for example, Holst's *The Planets* or Wagner's *The Valkyrie*; CD player or tape recorder.

What to do
● Ask the children to sit in a large circle and to shut their eyes.
● Explain that you are going to play a piece of dramatic instrumental music.
● Before you start the music, tell them that they are to listen quietly and that there is to be no interruption.
● When the music has finished, ask the children how the music made them feel. Did it make them think of anything? What did they visualise in their minds?
● Explain to the children that instrumental music can conjure up many different feelings and emotions. Share with the children what the music means to you. For example, *I felt like I was running away from something very scary and that I needed to escape quickly.*
● Encourage the children to express what they felt.
● Explain to the children that you are going to play the piece of music again and that you would like them to imagine that they are in a battle between good and evil.
● Encourage the children to think about the pitch of the music (whether it is high or low) and the dynamics (whether it is loud or soft). Do the changes in pitch and dynamic affect how they feel?
● When the music has finished, listen to some of the children's examples of what happened in their battle and what it involved.
● Pick four of the examples and divide the class into four groups of seven or eight. Allocate the children whose battles have been chosen as the leaders of these groups.
● Explain that you want each group to perform their leader's battle to the music. They will have ten minutes of preparation time and the leader's task is to direct the piece.
● Walk around the room observing their work.
● Invite the groups to take turns to perform their work in front of the class.

Differentiation
With less able children, allow more rehearsal time. Encourage more able children to make use of their bodies, and to express the emotions and feelings they want to convey through their faces.

AGE RANGE 7–9

LEARNING OBJECTIVES
To present animals through movement; to respond to a piece of music.

CURRICULUM LINKS
Music KS2: 1c, 3a.
QCA Music: Unit 9 – Exploring descriptive sounds.

Animal behaviour

What you need

'Animal behaviour' photocopiable page 67 (one copy for each child); safe, open space; CD or cassette of instrumental music that will make the children think of animals in the jungle; CD or cassette player.

What to do

● Ask the children to sit in a large circle and to shut their eyes.

● Explain that you are going to play a piece of instrumental music. You would like them to listen quietly and there is to be no interruption. You want them to think of animals moving around the jungle. Tell them to really think about what the animals look like and how they move.

● Play the music and afterwards, ask the children what animals they thought of.

● Share with the children what animal you thought of, and demonstrate how you think that animal moves, for example, a lion prowls, a monkey has long arms and uses these to swing through the trees.

● Encourage the children to enter the circle individually and share with the rest of the group how their animal moves.

● Give one copy of the 'Animal behaviour' photocopiable sheet to each child. Explain that you would like them to either choose one of the animals from the sheet and to answer the questions for that animal, or to draw a picture of the animal they have already chosen and answer the questions.

● When the children have completed the sheet, explain that you are going to play the music again and that you want them to move around the room imagining that they are the animals they have chosen, and that they are in the jungle looking for food.

● Emphasise that you do not want them to make sounds – they must present their animal through movement.

● Give the children five minutes of preparation time to work on their movements and then play the music.

● Encourage the children to concentrate on their animal's rhythm and pace, and discourage sounds.

Differentiation

Encourage more able children to concentrate on the rhythm of their animals and the patterns in the movement of their animals.

Drama and Role-play

AGE RANGE 8–9

LEARNING OBJECTIVES
To look at the use of sound in drama; to explore different arrangements of rhythms and noises.

CURRICULUM LINKS
Music KS2: 1a, 2a, 2b, 4a, 5c.
QCA Music: Unit 10 – Exploring rhythm and patterns;
Unit 11 – Exploring arrangements.

The factory

What you need
Safe, open space; whiteboard or flipchart; pens; whistle.

What to do
● Invite the children to sit in a large circle. Ask them if they know what a factory is. Can they suggest different types of products that are made in factories?

● Tell them that factories have different machines to make products. Choose a product and ask what machines might be involved in making it.

● Write suggestions for each stage of the factory process on the board.

● Explain that the machines make different rhythmic noises and movements.

● Demonstrate a couple of noises and movements, for example, the ticking of a machine and a boiler letting off steam. Then encourage children to think of other rhythmic movements and noises, which might be made by the machines producing their chosen product.

● Walk around the circle, making sure that every child thinks of a noise and a movement.

● Ask each child in turn to demonstrate their sound and movement. Ensure that each stage of the process is covered.

● Explain that you would now like them to become the factory production line. Work out which order their sounds and movements should go in, so that they follow each stage of the factory process.

● Ask the first child in the process to repeat their noise and movement in the centre of the circle. They will start the production line.

● Walk around the circle encouraging each child in turn to introduce his or her noise and movement. Make sure that every child's noise and movement is involved, and that they fit in time with the original rhythm.

● When the factory is up and running, ask the children to pause. Explain that you are going to conduct the level of volume by raising your arms above your head to indicate an increase and dropping them to indicate a decrease.

● Begin the exercise again, allowing a couple of minutes of preparation time.

● Use the whistle to signify closing time.

Differentiation
If the class is large, divide the group into two and allow one group to observe the other. By doing this, the exercise will become more structured and you are less likely to lose the rhythm. With more able children, emphasise the importance of sticking to the original rhythm. Encourage them to develop the rhythm of the movements as well as the sound.

AGE RANGE 9–11

LEARNING OBJECTIVES
To learn how to sing a round; to think about actions that accompany lyrics.

CURRICULUM LINKS
Music KS2: 1a, 1c.
QCA Music: Unit 17 – Roundabout – Exploring rounds.

Fire! Fire!

What you need
Copies of 'Fire! Fire!' photocopiable page 68.

What to do
● Hand out copies of the 'Fire! Fire' photocopiable sheet.
● Ask the children if they know the song and its tune.
● Sing the song with the children, so they become used to singing together.
● Divide the class into four groups, labelling them 'A', 'B', 'C' and 'D'.
● Tell the children that they are going to sing the song on the sheet as a musical round. Ask the children if they know what this means? (A song for different parts, each part singing the same song but starting at different times.)
● Explain how the round works. Group A starts singing the song. When group A finishes the first line (*London's burning! London's burning!*) group B start to sings, while group A carries on. When group B finish the first line, group C starts to sing, and when group C finish the first line, group D start to sing.
● Explain that all the groups must sing the song all the way through twice, and that group D will be the last group left singing.
● When the children are comfortable with singing in a round, encourage them to start adding the actions shown on the sheet.
● When they have practised with the actions, tell them you are going to conduct the level of volume of their round. You will raise your arms above your head to indicate an increase in volume and lower your arms to indicate a decrease the volume.
● Practise the round two or three times, bringing in each group at the right time.
Then ask each group to perform their round to the other groups in turn with the actions.

Differentiation
Less able children may need more time to learn the movements on the sheet and to incorporate these into the performance of the round.

Drama and
Role-play

AGE RANGE 10–11

LEARNING OBJECTIVES
To compose and perform a song; to understand the relationship between lyrics and melody.

CURRICULUM LINKS
Music KS2: 1a, 1c, 2a, 2b, 5a, 5c.
QCA Music: Unit 19 – Exploring lyrics and melody.

A new song

What you need
'A new song' photocopiable page 69 (one copy for each group); whiteboard or flipchart; pens.

What to do
● Ask the children for examples of songs that they like and know well. These might include songs they sing at school or current pop songs. Write down their suggestions on the board.
● When you have written about a dozen titles, read the list out.
● Explain to the children that you would like them to choose one of the songs from the list, making sure that they know the lyrics and the tune to the song.
● Divide the children into mixed-ability groups of three or four,

and give each group a copy of 'A new song' photocopiable sheet.
● Ask them to look at the top half of the sheet. Sing 'We Wish You a Merry Christmas' with them. Then explain that the environmental song next to it has different words, but the tune is the same. Sing the environmental song together, so they get the idea.
● Now ask them to look at the bottom half of the sheet. Explain that you would like them, in their groups, to write down the lyrics of the song they have chosen from the list on the board on the left-hand side of the page.
● When the groups have done this, explain that you would like them to think of new words to the same tune, with an environmental theme. They should write the new song down on the right-hand side of the page.
● Emphasise that the original tune stays the same, it is only the words that change.
● Tell the children to look at the environmental song that has been written to the tune of 'We Wish You a Merry Christmas' to help them.
● Give the children 20 minutes to complete the task.
● When they have finished, allow each group in turn to perform their songs to the rest of the class. Encourage positive feedback from the children watching.

Differentiation
Less able children will need more guidance in thinking about lyrics and matching them to the melody of their chosen song. Allow more able children to develop this exercise by looking at other themes.

Drama and Role-play

AGE RANGE 10–11

LEARNING OBJECTIVE
To practise performing in front of an audience; to compose a song.

CURRICULUM LINKS
Music KS2: 1a, 1c, 3b, 2b, 5c.
QCA Music: Unit 20 – Performing together.

The concert

What you need
Safe, open space; pens; paper.

What to do
● Divide the class into groups of five or six. Allocate a leader to each group and give them a pen and a few sheets of paper.
● Explain that they will be devising an original piece of music with lyrics.
● Ask the groups to decide on a theme for the song, such as war, friendship or sport. Allow the children a couple of minutes for this.
● The group should then write lyrics for a verse of a song based on that theme. They could begin by noting down words they associate with the theme they have chosen. Encourage them to keep the lyrics simple.
● Once they have their verse, they should work out their song's pace and rhythm. The words of the lyrics may suggest rhythms that could be used.
● The leader should set the pace by clapping at a moderate speed. Then, the other children can experiment with different rhythms, until they come up with patterns that they would like to use.
● When they have decided on a rhythm, they can begin to devise a melody. Remind them to think about their lyrics and the theme of their song. Will their melody be happy or sad? Calm or exciting?
● Finally, ask the children to practise performing their songs. Walk around the room, making sure that they are on the right track.
● When the children have finished practising, invite the groups, in turn, to perform their songs.
● When all the groups have performed, ask the children to take a vote on which was their favourite song.
● When a winning song has been chosen, ask the leader to teach the song to the remaining groups.

Differentiation
With less able children, place the emphasis on getting the pace and rhythm right, and keeping the lyrics simple. Encourage more able children to experiment with sound and to work on more than one verse.

Drama and
Role-play

BRIGHT
IDEAS

Animal behaviour

Am I fast or slow?

What do I look like?

How do I move?

Am I fast or slow?

What do I look like?

How do I move?

Am I fast or slow?

What do I look like?

How do I move?

My animal choice:

Am I fast or slow?

What do I look like?

How do I move?

Fire! Fire!

London's burning!

London's burning!

Fetch the engine!

Fetch the engine!

Fire! Fire!

Fire! Fire!

Pour on water!

Pour on water!

Drama and
Role-play

A new song

<u>We Wish You a Merry Christmas</u>

We wish you a merry Christmas,
We wish you a merry Christmas,
We wish you a merry Christmas
And a happy New Year!

Glad tidings we bring,
To you and your kin,
We wish you a merry Christmas
And a happy New Year!

<u>An environmental song</u>
(Sung to the tune of 'We Wish You a Merry Christmas')

We wish for a cleaner planet,
We wish for a cleaner planet,
We wish for a cleaner planet
And pollution-free air!

Glad rulings we bring,
To you and your kin,
We wish for a cleaner planet
And pollution-free air!

My chosen song

_____

_____

_____

_____

_____

_____

_____

_____

_____

My new song, sung to the tune of

_____

_____

_____

_____

_____

_____

_____

_____

_____

CHAPTER 6

Religious education

AGE RANGE 5–8

LEARNING OBJECTIVES
To encourage storytelling through looking at pictures from a church; to learn about some of the activities that take place in a church.

CURRICULUM LINKS
Religious education KS1: 1b, 1c, 3a, 3l.
QCA RE: Unit 1F – What can we learn from visiting a church?

In a church

What you need
Copies of 'In a church' photocopiable page 80; safe, open space; whiteboard or flipchart; pens.

What to do
● Hand out the 'In a church' photocopiable sheet, making sure that each child can see a copy comfortably.
● Ask the children to look at the pictures on the sheet and explain what they see. For example, *I see a man and woman getting married and the vicar is blessing them.*
● Explain that each picture shows an act that takes place in a church: a wedding, a christening and a funeral. Have the children ever experienced one of these ceremonies? Encourage them to share their experiences.
● Share with the children your thoughts on what a church represents to you. For example, *a quiet place, peaceful, stained glass windows, hymn books, smells old* and so on.
● Write some of your thoughts on the board. Ask the children to call out their ideas and add them to the list.
● Divide the class into smaller groups.
● Explain that you would like them to choose one of the pictures from the sheet and rehearse a small sketch, demonstrating what the people in the pictures are doing.
● Explain that you would like the sketch to be informative. They need to explain what is taking place and what it means.
● Give the children ten minutes of preparation time.
● Walk around the room, making sure that the children are on the right track.
● Invite the groups, in turn, to come to the front of the class and share their work.
● At the end of each group's performance offer constructive criticism, making sure that you pick up on any areas that were not covered, for example, wedding vows, prayers or blessings.
● Ensure that the children understand that they are imagining they are in a special place and need to be respectful in their behaviour.

Differentiation
With less able children, encourage the storytelling aspect so that they understand why these ceremonies are important. Make sure that more able children investigate the three ceremonies in depth.

Drama and
Role-play
BRIGHT IDEAS

Word batting

AGE RANGE 5–8

LEARNING OBJECTIVES
To improvise; to think about words associated with festivals.

CURRICULUM LINKS
Religious education KS1 and KS2: 1a, 1b, 2a, 3g.
QCA RE: Unit 2c – Celebrations.

What you need
Safe, open space; whiteboard or flipchart; pens.

What to do
● Invite the children to sit in a circle.
● Ask them if they know what a celebration is. Can they give examples of different celebrations? These can be special occasions or festivals. Write their ideas on the whiteboard.
● Tell the children that they are going to play a simple word game that will test their knowledge of celebrations.
● Demonstrate how the game works using two volunteers. Invite them to sit cross-legged opposite each other in the centre of the circle. Explain that you are going to give the pair a topic and they have to 'bat' words associated with that topic back and forth to each other. For example, if the topic was dinners, it could go like this: *roast chicken – lasagne – spaghetti bolognaise – sausage and mash – fish and chips*. The first one to hesitate or stop is out.
● Play the game with the volunteers. Then tell the children that they will play the game using the topic 'Celebrations'.
● Brainstorm words, ideas and themes that are associated with celebrations and write them on the board.
● Encourage the children to think about all the things associated with celebrations, such as moods, artefacts, actions, special foods, activities and symbols.
● Explain to the children it will be a class competition for who can stay in the circle for the longest.
● Invite the first pair up and ask the rest of the class to be quiet. As soon as one person is out, invite the next pair to come up and start a new word-batting game.
● Keep score on the whiteboard as to who stayed in the game the longest and who was the first to hesitate.

Differentiation
With less able children, allow more pausing time so that they can get into the swing of the game and feel confident within it. With more able children, keep the winner of the first word batting game in the circle, introduce a new opponent and see who can stay in the circle the longest while continuing to introduce new opponents.

AGE RANGE 6–8

LEARNING OBJECTIVES
To think about appropriate words in storytelling; to understand why the Torah is important.

CURRICULUM LINKS
Religious education KS1 and KS2: 1a, 2a, 2e, 3f.
QCA RE: Unit 2A – What is the Torah and why is it important to Jewish people?

One at a time

What you need
Safe, open space; whiteboard or flipchart; pens.

What to do
● Ask the children to sit in a circle.
● Explain that you would like them to think about the Jewish faith.
● Ask the children what are the first words that come to mind when thinking about the Jewish faith. Give a few examples, *God, ark, Torah, faith* and so on.
● Write their suggested words on the board under the heading, 'The Jewish faith'.
● Next, focus the children on the Torah and why it is important to Jewish people. (It is a special book that teaches Jewish people how to live.)
● Tell the children that they are going to tell a story, collectively as a class, explaining why the Torah is important to Jewish people.
● The story will be delivered as a 'one-word story'. The storytelling moves around the circle and each child is only allowed to say one word at a time.
● Tell the children that they can have one practice-run by telling a short story that they devise themselves.
● Start the story off, for example, your opening words could be *Once, There* or *I.*
● The children will have to concentrate and make sure that the words fit together well.
● If a child's word does not fit, stop the exercise and ask the rest of the class if they know of any words that would be more suitable.
● Once you feel that the exercise has been fully understood, explain to the children that they are now going to tell the story of why the Torah is important to Jewish people.
● Emphasise to the children that they need to pay attention to what is being said to continue the story.
● The exercise can be repeated if you feel that their knowledge on the subject needs to be refined.

Differentiation
Less able children are more likely to need guidance through the exercise. It may also be helpful to write their words on the board as the story moves around the circle. Encourage more able children to think about sentence structure and to say more, depending on their knowledge.

Drama and Role-play

AGE RANGE 6–11

LEARNING OBJECTIVES
To look at the importance of plot; to look at the story of Noah.

CURRICULUM LINKS
Religious education KS1 and KS2: 1a, 3f.
QCA RE: Unit 2A – What is the Torah and why is it important to Jewish people?; Unit 3D – What is the Bible and why is it important for Christians?

Film trailer

What you need
'Film trailer' photocopiable page 81 (one copy for each child); safe, open space.

What to do
● Hand out the 'Film trailer' photocopiable sheet and ask the children to describe what they see.
● Invite them to share their ideas and thoughts about the story of 'Noah and the Ark'.
● Ask the children to write down answers to the questions in the bubbles.
● When they have finished, divide the children into groups. Tell each group to imagine that it is making a film about 'Noah' and to create a film trailer.
● Ask the children if they know what a film trailer is. Encourage them to back up their examples with evidence. For example, *A film trailer is small advert about a film that does not give the plot away.*
● Explain that the children's trailer must show three important pieces of action from the story of 'Noah'. It must also involve a narrator, who will tell the audience what to expect from the film. The trailer must start with the words, *In cinemas from September….*
● Give the children 15 minutes of preparation time.
● Walk around the groups making sure that they are on the right track.
● Invite the first group to come to the front of the class and perform its trailer.
● At the end of each trailer, invite constructive criticism from the rest of the group.

Differentiation
Less able children should concentrate more on the plot of 'Noah'. Make sure that they understand the story fully. Encourage more able children to be adventurous, by using sound effects and different accents.

 Drama and Role-play

AGE RANGE 7–9

LEARNING OBJECTIVES
To look at different religious celebrations; to speak with conviction and understanding.

CURRICULUM LINKS
Religious education KS2: 1a, 1b, 2a, 3g.
QCA RE: Unit 2c – Celebrations; Unit 3B – How and why do Hindus celebrate Divali?; Unit 4B – Celebrations: Christmas journeys; Unit 4C – Why is Easter important for Christians?

Let's celebrate

What you need
'Let's celebrate' photocopiable page 82 (one copy for each child); pens or pencils.

What to do
● Explain that many people have religious beliefs that they feel strongly about. Share your own feelings about a special occasion celebrated by a religious faith. For example, *I think it is a great idea that the Muslim faith celebrates with Eid after the fasting of Ramadan.*

● Give a brief speech to explain why the occasion you have chosen is good to celebrate. Maintain eye-contact with the children, use gesture for emphasis and incorporate oral techniques to retain their attention, for example, vary your pace or use rhetorical language.

● Ask the children to suggest religious celebrations that they enjoy, for example, Christmas or Divali, and to explain how these celebrations originated.

● Point out that when we have something that we want to celebrate, we want to share that happiness with others. Tell the children that they are going to plan a speech to encourage others to celebrate with them, by telling them all about the celebration and why it is a good idea.

● Explain that the talk should last for approximately one minute. Give them a guideline of about 150 words.

● Hand out copies of the 'Let's celebrate' photocopiable sheet, explaining how the children can use the sheet to help plan their talk.

● Allow the children to practise their talk with a partner. Remind them of the techniques of audience eye-contact and speaking up.

● When everyone is ready, invite the children to make their speeches to the group.

● At the end of each talk, invite constructive criticism from the rest of the group. Point out where they could have improved their speech, or any areas they forgot to cover.

Differentiation
Allow less able children to spend more time exploring the different types of celebration so that they feel comfortable with the topic. If the children are young, allow them to deliver their work in pairs. Introduce heckling during the speeches of more able children, so that they have to make a strong argument.

Drama and
Role-play

AGE RANGE 7–9

LEARNING OBJECTIVES
To look at the meaning of signs and symbols; to interpret a message through stillness.

CURRICULUM LINKS
Religious education KS2: 1e, 3i.
QCA RE: Unit 3A – What do signs and symbols mean?

My sign

What you need
Safe, open space; whiteboard or flipchart; pens.

What to do
● Ask the children to sit in a circle.
● Explain that they will be looking at the use of signs and symbols, and what they mean.
● Ask the children what signs or symbols they have come across. What did the signs and symbols mean? Prompt them with ideas, for example, road and traffic signs, or signs in restaurants.
● Share some of the signs that you come across everyday, for example, speed limits or 'no smoking' signs, and draw them on the board.
● Invite the children to draw more signs on the board.
● Explain that signs and symbols are also used in connection with religion. Can the children think of any religious signs or symbols? Where have the children seen them and what do they mean? For example, a cross represents the death of Jesus Christ: you can find crosses in churches and sometimes people wear them around their necks.
● Encourage the children to give examples and ask them for evidence. Make sure that signs from many faiths are included in the discussion, such as the Star of David from the Jewish faith, and the five 'Ks' from the Sikh faith.
● Divide the class into groups of four or five.
● Tell each group that you would like them to choose a different religious faith, for example, Christianity, Sikhism, Muslim or Jewish.
● Explain to the groups that you would like them to mould their bodies into a new sign or symbol that represents their chosen faith, or an aspect of it.
● Give the children five minutes of preparation time.
● Invite each group, in turn, to share their work. At the end of each demonstration, ask the children to explain what their sign represents.

Differentiation
Allow less able children more discussion time about signs and symbols, and investigate further examples and their meanings. With more able children, allow longer preparation time for the new sign activity.

 Drama and Role-play

AGE RANGE 7–11

LEARNING OBJECTIVES
To look at parables in the Gospel; to create a sketch setting a parable in a modern-day context.

CURRICULUM LINKS
Religious education KS2: 1a, 1b, 2c, 3f.
QCA RE: Unit 2B – Why did Jesus tell stories?; Unit 3C – What do we know about Jesus?; Unit 3D – What is the Bible and why is it important for Christians?

Modern-day parable

What you need
'Modern-day parables' photocopiable page 83 (one copy for each child); pens or pencils.

What to do
● Tell the children that the Gospels are part of the Bible. They tell of the life of Jesus. An important part of the Gospels are the parables. These are stories that Jesus told to teach people about his new faith. Each of the parables has a message within it.

● Ask the children if they can think of any examples of parables. Discuss a few well-known parables, such as 'The Good Samaritan' or 'The Prodigal Son', giving a brief outline of the story and discussing the 'message' in each.

● Divide the class into groups of four or five.

● Explain that you would like the groups to choose one of the parables from the Gospels and make a modern-day version of it. For example, an updated version of 'The Good Samaritan' might have an old woman being robbed. Several people pass who might be expected to help, but it is the most 'unlikely' character who gives the old woman some money and takes her to the police station.

● Using their sheets, ask the children to fill in the examples they have chosen and to choose what elements of the story they would like to represent.

● Allow the children 20 minutes of rehearsal time.

● Walk around the room making sure that the children are on the right track. Provide further guidance if necessary.

● Invite the groups to perform their stories in front of the class, and encourage the others to guess which story they have adapted.

● Ask the children to give each group constructive criticism when they have finished performing their parable.

Differentiation
Less able children should spend more time getting the story's message across. Encourage more able children to concentrate on how the story is told and develop characterisation.

76

Drama and Role-play

AGE RANGE 8–10

LEARNING OBJECTIVES
To look at the importance of plot, expression and gesture in drama; to look at the Christmas story.

CURRICULUM LINKS
Religious education KS2: 1a, 1b, 3f, 3g.
QCA RE: Unit 4B – Christmas journeys.

Christmas story

What you need
Safe, open space; whiteboard or flipchart; pens.

What to do
- Ask the children to sit in a circle.
- Explain that they will be looking at the story of Christmas and what it really means.
- Ask the children to think of words that they associate with Christmas, for example, *Father Christmas*, *presents*, *tree*, *Baby Jesus* and so on. Write the words on the board.
- Ask the children if they know the story behind Christmas (the nativity and the birth of Jesus).
- Divide the class into groups of four and five.
- Explain that, in their groups, they will be devising a small play about Christmas. All the action in the play must be mimed. There will be a narrator and different members of the group should take turns in this role. Emphasise that the story must be easy to follow. If someone did not know the Christmas story, or could not speak the English language, they should still be able to follow the story by seeing the play.
- Give the groups 20 minutes of preparation time.
- Walk around the class, making sure that the groups are on the right track and that they are sticking to the guidelines.
- Invite the groups to come to the front of the class and share their plays.
- Give feedback where you think necessary.

Differentiation
With less able children, make sure that the story is kept simple. Ask more able children to introduce feelings, mood and expression in their work. Encourage them to investigate how the characters must have felt.

Drama and Role-play

Speaker's corner

AGE RANGE 9–11

LEARNING OBJECTIVES
To think about the importance of special books in religion; to focus on the Qur'an; to work on confidence in public speaking.

CURRICULUM LINKS
Religious education KS2: 1a, 1b, 1c, 2a, 2c, 3f, 3g, 3k, 3l. QCA RE: Unit 6D – What is the Qur'an and why is it important to Muslims?

What you need
Safe, open space.

What to do
● Ask the children to sit in a circle.
● Explain that many people have religious beliefs that they feel strongly about. Share your own feelings about a religious belief. For example, *I think it is a great idea that the Christians have the Bible because it reminds them of events that took place in the past.*
● Go on to explain your feelings further. Maintain eye-contact with the children, using gesture for emphasis and oral techniques to retain their attention, for example, vary your pace or use rhetorical language.
● Tell the children that some religions have special books.
● Ask them what they know about any special religious books, and why they are important.
● When you have heard their examples, focus on the Qur'an and encourage the children to think about why this book is important to the Muslim faith. For example, it is a book of guidance and it teaches that God has many qualities.
● Tell the children about Speaker's Corner in Hyde Park, London. Explain that it is a place where people can say exactly what they think. Anyone is free to have their say, although some listeners may heckle if they disagree.
● Explain to the children that you would like them all, individually, to get up in front of the class and explain why they think the Qur'an is important.
● Ask the children to plan their talks, which should last about one minute. Give them a guideline of about 150 words.
● Walk around the room, giving help where necessary.
● Allow the children to practise their talk with a partner. Remind them of the techniques of audience eye-contact and speaking up.
● When everyone is ready, invite the children to make their speeches to the group.
● At the end of each talk, invite constructive criticism from the rest of the group. Point out where they could have improved their speech, or areas they forgot to cover.

Differentiation
Allow less able children to spend more time writing the speech. If the children are young, allow them to deliver their speech in pairs. Encourage more able children to carry out in-depth research, looking at the Qur'an history, and introduce heckling.

Drama and Role-play

AGE RANGE 9–11

LEARNING OBJECTIVE
To learn the importance of mime and movement in drama; to look at the expression of faith through art.

CURRICULUM LINKS
Religious education KS2: 1e, 2a, 3i, 3r.
QCA RE: Unit 6F – How do people express faith through the arts?

Silent movie

What you need
'Silent movie' photocopiable page 84; CD or cassette of religious, classical music, such as Handel's *Messiah*; CD or cassette player.

What to do
● Ask the children to sit in a circle.
● Explain to them that people who are religious will express their faith by going to a church, mosque or synagogue.
● Sometimes people also express their faith through the arts, for example, they might paint religious pictures or compose religious music. Ask the children to think of examples of religious art or music that they have seen or heard.
● Hand out copies of the 'Silent movie' photocopiable sheet and ask the children to describe what they see. Can they think of other ways that people express their faith through the arts? What do they do? How do they conduct themselves? Encourage the children to give evidence with their examples.
● Divide the class into groups of four or five.
● Invite the groups to listen to the piece of classical music that you have chosen.
● At the end of the piece, ask what kind of emotions the music conjured up for them.
● Explain that you would like each group to devise a piece of silent theatre, demonstrating a faith that they have studied. The piece must be in mime with no talking. The music will be played throughout their piece.
● Allocate a faith to each group, for example, Jewish, Muslim and Christian.
● Allow the group to talk about what aspects of that faith they would like to show and how they are going to show them.
● Share with the children your thoughts on what they could demonstrate. For example, praying to God will lead you to heaven.
● Give the children 15 minutes of preparation time.
● Walk around the room, making sure that they are on the right track.
● Keep the classical music playing, to spur on their imaginations.
● At the end of the rehearsal time, invite the first group to come to the front of the class and perform.

Differentiation
With less able children, spend more time on looking at the expression of faith through the arts, making sure that they understand the concept.

Drama and Role-play

In a church

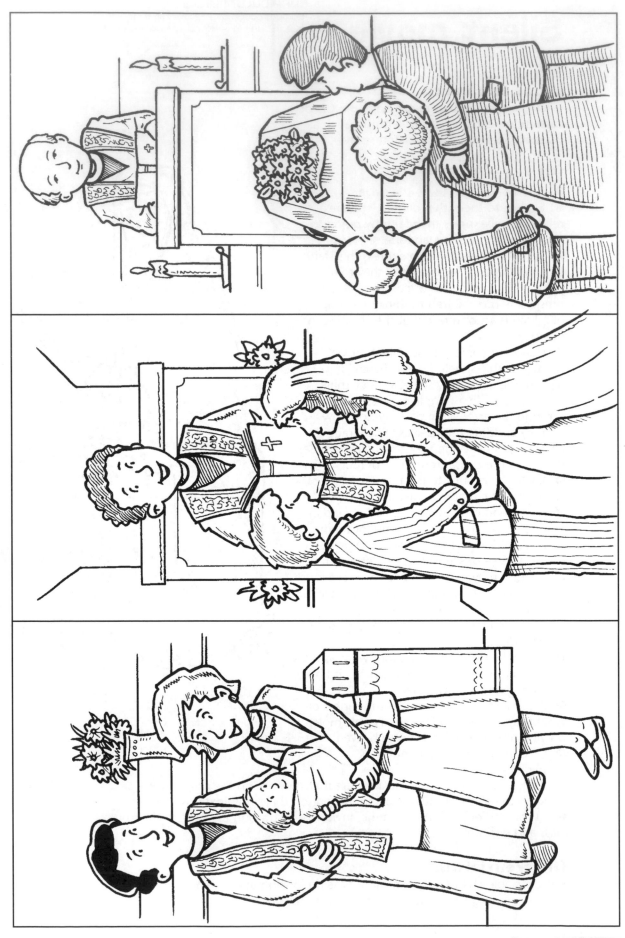

Drama and
Role-play

Film trailer

Who was Noah?

What did he do and why?

Where did he go?

Where did he come from?

Let's celebrate

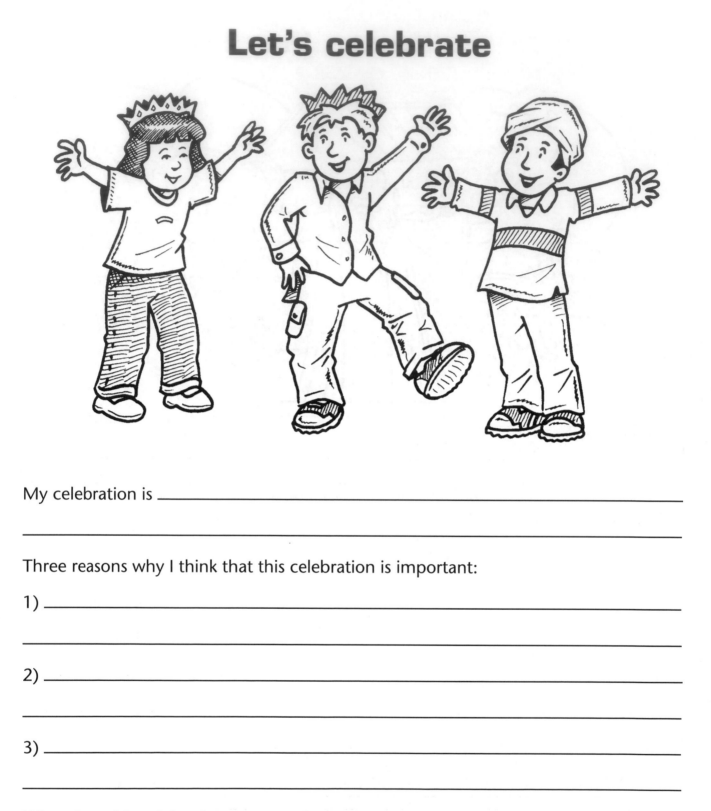

My celebration is _____

_____

Three reasons why I think that this celebration is important:

1) _____

_____

2) _____

_____

3) _____

_____

What does this celebration represent? _____

_____

How did this celebration originate? _____

_____

Drama and
Role-play

Modern-day parables

The parable we have chosen from the Gospels is _____

_____

This is what happens in the parable: _____

_____

_____

_____

_____

_____

_____

_____

Our modern-day setting will be _____

_____

Our modern-day characters will be _____

_____

_____

We will make the story modern by _____

_____

_____

_____

_____

_____

_____

_____

_____

Silent movie

Drama and
Role-play

CHAPTER 7

Physical education

AGE RANGE 5–9

LEARNING OBJECTIVES
To dance expressively and balance well; to learn the importance of movement and stillness in drama.

CURRICULUM LINKS
Physical education KS1 and KS2: 1b, 6a, 6c, 8a. QCA PE: Unit 1 – Dance activities (1); Unit 2 – Dance activities (2); Unit 3 – Games activities (1); Unit 4 – Games activities (2).

Musical statues

What you need
Safe, open space; CD or cassette of music; CD or cassette player.

What to do
● Ask the children to find a space on the floor where they can stand comfortably and move their arms around in a circle without touching anyone else.
● Explain that you will play some music and that you would like them to dance, on their own, making sure that they move all parts of their bodies.
● When the music stops, tell them to stand as still as a statue: the only parts of their body that are allowed to move are their eyes (for blinking).
● Explain to the children

that while they are statues, you will be walking around the space looking at them, making sure that they do not move. If they move, they are out, and have to sit down on the floor.
● Allow the children a couple of practice-runs before you start.
● Encourage them to dance expressively by saying that you will be giving an award to the most expressive dancer. Encourage the boys in the competition and say that boys' dancing is a very good thing.
● Emphasise to the children that this is a PE lesson and that you would like to see them move all parts of their bodies. Those children who are shy could perhaps dance with a friend to begin with.
● Once you are satisfied that each child knows what they are doing, play the game.
● Introduce a new element to the game. When the music stops and you walk around the room, try to make the children laugh. If they laugh, they have to sit down.

Differentiation
Encourage more able children to move expressively and challenge them by stopping the music when they are particularly animated, checking their sense of balance.

AGE RANGE 6–8

LEARNING OBJECTIVES
To play a 'role-playing' game; to use skills, strategies and tactics to outwit the opposition.

CURRICULUM LINKS
Physical education KS1 and KS2: 2b, 7a, 7b, 7c.
QCA PE: Unit 4 – Games activities (2); Unit 10 – Invasion games (1); Unit 11 – Invasion games (2).

Pirates

What you need
Safe, open space; four PE mats; skittles (a number divisible by four); bands in four different colours; labels for the mats, in colours that match the bands.

What to do
● Place a PE mat in each corner of the room and name or label each mat a different colour.
● Place an equal number of skittles on each mat.
● Explain to the children that they will be playing a game called 'Pirates'.
● Pick four children to be 'ships'. Divide the rest of the children into four teams of 'pirates' and give each team bands of a different colour. Each team has an 'island' (one of the mats, the colour of which matches the team's bands).
● The skittles on the 'islands' are 'treasures'. The object of the game is for the pirates to place as many treasures as they can on their team's island. Each pirate can only pick up one treasure at a time.
● The four 'ships' have to try to tag the pirates. They can only go on the sea in between the islands.
● The pirates are safe when they are on an island. But each island can only hold a maximum of six pirates at any one time and only for a period of ten seconds.
● If a pirate is out, they must sit out of the game. If they are holding a treasure, that object is also taken out of the game.
● Start the game by putting a mix of children from different groups on each mat.
● Emphasise that they must play safely and be careful while they are running around.
● To avoid conflict, emphasise that there is to be no snatching or arguing over the treasures.
● The last four pirates to survive at the end of the game (after ten minutes) are the winners. They get a bonus if their team island holds the most treasures.

Differentiation
With less able children, allow more time on the mats and remove the element of the 'treasures' for a more straightforward game. With more able children, you can shorten the length of the time on the mats to add an element of drama to the game.

Drama and Role-play

AGE RANGE 7–9

LEARNING OBJECTIVE
To develop basic fitness techniques for drama; to learn to listen carefully and to follow instructions.

CURRICULUM LINKS
Physical education KS1: 1a, 1c, 2c; KS2: 10a, 10b, 10c. QCA PE: Unit 18 – Athletic activities (2).

Apple, pear, banana

What you need
Safe, open space.

What to do
● Ask the class to stand in a large circle.
● Walk around the outside of the circle labelling the children 'apple', 'pear' or 'banana'. Ideally, there should be an equal number of each fruit.
● Ask the children to listen carefully while you explain the rules of the game.
● Explain that you will call out either *Apple!*, *Pear!* or *Banana!*. When you do, those children must run clockwise around the outside of the circle. When you shout *Change!*, the children must change direction. When you shout *Home!*, the children must continue running in the same direction and get back to their original place as quickly as possible.
● The last child to return 'home' is out, and sits down in their place while the game continues.
● Explain that when a few children are out, you will call out a couple of fruit names, and both groups must run together, still following the rules of the game. The last child left in is the winner.
● You could introduce a competitive element by playing the game a few times over the term and keeping a record of which team wins each time. The team with the most wins at the end of the term is the overall winner.
● If you see that some of the children are becoming exhausted, introduce shorter lengths of running time and try to make sure that you do not call out the same fruit more than twice.

Differentiation
This activity is a good warm-up exercise to encourage the children to listen carefully and follow instructions. With less able children, make sure that you explain the game so that everyone fully understands what is happening. You may need to give a demonstration. With more able children, raise the stakes by introducing a competition format or changing the instructions to encompass other movements.

Drama and Role-play

AGE RANGE 8–11

LEARNING OBJECTIVES
To build on fitness levels and co-ordination;
to encourage group bonding and team work.

CURRICULUM LINKS
Physical education KS2: 8a, 8b, 10a, 10b, 10c.
QCA PE: Unit 14 – Gymnastic activities (3); Unit 17
– Athletic activities (1).

Crazy chase

What you need
Safe, open space; piece of chalk.

What to do
● Divide the class into two teams, labelling them 'A' and 'B'.
● Draw a chalk line at one end of the room to represent a starting line. Draw another chalk line at the other end of the room to represent the halfway mark.
● Ask the two groups to stand behind the starting line.
● Tell the children that they will be running a relay race. Explain that only one person is allowed to run at a time. Each child runs from the starting point to the halfway mark and then back again to the starting point, allowing the next runner to leave.
● Encourage all of the children to participate, reminding them that the game is about speed and skill.
● When the two teams have practised the relay by running, introduce some variations, for example, the first, fourth, seventh and tenth runners in each team must move sideways, the second, fifth, eighth and eleventh runners must walk pigeon-toed, and the third, sixth, ninth and twelfth runners must hop. If the team members forget how they have to travel their team is disqualified.
● Allow a couple of practice-runs before you actually start the game.
● To encourage group bonding, allow the children to cheer for each other. You could also organise a competition – the best team over three full relays is the winner.

Differentiation
Take into account the children's ages before you set the type of runs. Always be aware of the safety aspects of the game. With less able children, start with simple running and then add the original goals. With more able children you can encourage more athletic walks or styles for the relay.

Drama and
Role-play

AGE RANGE 8–11

LEARNING OBJECTIVE
To learn the importance of being a team player (in sport and in drama).

CURRICULUM LINKS
Physical education KS2: 8a, 8b, 10a, 10b, 10c, 11b, 11c.
QCA PE: Unit 28 – Gymnastic activities (6).

Crossing the river

What you need
Safe, open space; piece of chalk; four small gym mats.

What to do
● Divide the class into two large groups and give each group two mats.

● With chalk, draw two lines at either end of the room.

● Ask the children to stand behind one of the lines.

● Allocate a responsible child to be the leader of each group.

● Tell the children that the space in between the two lines is the river and the space behind the lines are the river banks.

● The leader of each group has two mats to take him or herself, and two other team mates, across the river. None of the children crossing are allowed to touch the floor and they can only use the mats to move across the room.

● Once they have got to the other river bank, the leader drops the two team mates off and travels back across the hall to pick up the

next two. After the last two team mates have been picked up, the leader gets off at the other bank with them. The first team back is the winner.

● The children can become very excitable during this activity, so ensure that you are in control of how the game is conducted. Make sure that the children understand that it is important to play safely and remind them that they must not pull a mat if someone is still on it.

● Explain to the children that the game is more about skill than speed. Allow them to have a quick practice-run before they start. To begin with, let them work out a way of getting across the river. If they are struggling, show them how to transfer from one mat to the other. Start the game when you think that the children have grasped the idea. Change the leaders after three journeys, as the game can become quite tiring.

Differentiation
With less able children, make sure that the rules are clear and that they realise they must not touch the floor. With more able children, add a chair or small piece apparatus in the river to act as an obstacle. This will make the exercise more testing.

AGE RANGE 9–11

LEARNING OBJECTIVES
To look at character and adrenalin in drama; to learn an 'invasion game'.

CURRICULUM LINKS
Physical education KS2: 7a, 7b, 7c.
QCA PE: Unit 11 – Invasion games (2).

Elves and wizards

What you need
Safe, open space; bands in two colours.

What to do
● Divide the children into two teams and give each team coloured bands.
● Ask both teams to stand in a long line, facing each other, at opposite ends of the room.
● Walk up the lines and name each child an elf or a wizard. Each team should be made up of one-third wizards and two-thirds elves.
● Give the children a quick practice to role-play their characters. Elves have to put their hands on their heads, wriggle their fingers and shout *Wee hee*. Wizards have to put their hands in their air and shout *Kapow!*
● Explain how the game works. You count from one to six and as you do so, the children move forward six steps. Then you say *Stop!* and the children stop in their tracks and role-play their characters. Say *Go!* and the game begins.
● The object of the game is for the elves on each team to get to the opposite side of the room. The wizards have to stop the elves on the opposite team by tagging them. When an elf has been tagged, he or she freezes. Elves can be saved by wizards on their own team tapping their shoulder.
● Make sure that you practise the game so that all the children are clear about the rules. Explain that the game will go better if they continue role-playing their characters as they play.

Differentiation
The number of elves and wizards will depend on the size of your class. If your class is very big, you may want to divide it into four teams, and have two games. The winning teams of each game could then play each other. Spend more time going over the rules with less able children. The game can be complicated to begin with, but very exciting to play.

Drama and Role-play

CHAPTER 8

Information and communication technology

Information and

AGE RANGE 5–8

LEARNING OBJECTIVES
To use and recognise key words to describe moods, to use our faces and bodies to convey a particular mood.

CURRICULUM LINKS
ICT KS1 and KS2: 2a, 3a.
QCA ICT: Unit 1D – Labelling and classifying.

The mood circle

What you need
Safe, open space; digital camera (optional).

What to do
● Ask the children to sit in a circle.
● Explain that our faces can sometimes express our emotional moods, for example, we smile when we are happy and we cry when we are sad.
● Ask the children to think of different emotional moods and encourage them to use their faces to give examples.
● Demonstrate a few emotions with your face, for example, happy, sad and excited. Can the children recognise the moods you are demonstrating? Can they give reasons for their choices?

● Explain that you would like the children to practise four mood faces of their own.
● Walk around the room, making sure that the children are on the right track.
● When the children have finished, ask them to stand in a circle.
● Move around the circle and ask the children, one by one, to demonstrate their four faces. The rest of the class have to guess the moods.
● Encourage the children to use as many descriptive words as they can to describe the mood or feeling that is being expressed.
● Explain to the children that you are going to shout out different names of moods, for example, *Jealous! Angry! Spiteful! Happy!* and so on. You will give a five second countdown before shouting out *Freeze!,* then the children must demonstrate that mood with their faces and bodies. For example, if you shouted *Angry!,* the children should use their faces and bodies to look really angry and aggressive.
● As an extension to the activity, ask for parental permission to use a digital camera to photograph different moods and expressions. You could also make labels using a word-processing program to create a 'mood display'.

Differentiation
Ask more able children to work in pairs to demonstrate different moods within a scenario. For example, child 1 could demonstrate kindness (giving a present) while child 2 demonstrates happiness (receiving the present).

AGE RANGE 6–9

LEARNING OBJECTIVES
To communicate ideas through text; to work together to produce a short sketch.

CURRICULUM LINKS
ICT KS1 and KS2: 2a, 2d, 3b.
QCA ICT: Unit 2A – Writing stories.

Choose your words

What you need
'Choose your words' photocopiable page 95 (one copy for each child); blank slips of paper; pens.

What to do
● Ask the children to sit down in a large circle.
● Hand out the slips of paper and pens, and ask the children to write down one word, which must be the name of an object, an animal, or a male or female name.
● When everyone has written a word, ask them to put their slips of paper in the centre of the circle so that everyone can see the words.
● Divide the class into groups of five, allocating a leader to each group. Ask the leader to pick up five of the words from the centre of the circle and to return to their group.
● Hand out the 'Choose your words' photocopiable sheet to each child and ask them to write down their group's words in the bubbles at the top.
● Explain to the children that they are going to devise a short sketch involving all of these words.
● Encourage the children to work together in their groups and to write any of their plot ideas on the sheet.
● Walk around the room, making sure that each group is on the right track. Explain to the children that you do not want the story to be complicated. The words that they have chosen do not all have to be a major part of the sketch.
● Allow them 15 minutes of preparation time.
● Invite each group, in turn, to the front of the class to perform their sketches.
● At the end of each sketch, open up a class discussion. The class should comment on whether the group made good use of their five words.
● Encourage constructive criticism from the rest of the class.
● Use the words from this session to develop a 'plot bag' for other improvised role-play games.

Differentiation
Make sure that less able children do not get confused when they plot their sketch. Encourage them to focus on possible links between their words. Allow more able children extra time if necessary, so that they can devise a good sketch.

Drama and Role-play

Famous name party game

AGE RANGE 7–11

LEARNING OBJECTIVES
To look at the use of logical questioning; to look at characterisation and to practise improvising.

CURRICULUM LINKS
ICT KS2: 1a, 3a.
QCA ICT: Unit 2E – Questions and answers; Unit 3C – Introduction to databases; Unit 4A – Writing for different audiences; Unit 4C – Branching databases.

What you need
Safe, open space.

What to do
● Ask the children to sit in a large circle.
● Explain to the children that they are going to play a game. It involves improvisation and is based around the theme of hosting a party.
● Ask for a volunteer to be the host of the party.
● Choose four children from the circle to be guests.
● Explain that you are going to give the four guests the identity of a famous character or person, for example, Sleeping Beauty, Goldilocks or Jack and the Beanstalk. The host and other children will not be told what characters the guests are going to be.
● The four guests have to walk into the centre of the circle (one at a time) as though they have just arrived at a party. It is the host's job to guess which character each guest is by asking questions.
● The guests have to pretend to be their characters but are not allowed at any point to say who they are.
● The host has two minutes to guess the identity of each guest. After this time, the other children in the circle can guess who they are. Anyone who guesses correctly will participate in the next round.
● Encourage the children to try hard at pretending that they are at a party and to work on their improvisation technique.
● Make sure that the characters you allocate are going to be recognised by most of the children.
● Have a quick practice-run with the children before you start the main game.
● Give the four chosen children their characters and allow them one minute to mentally prepare before the game begins.
● At the end of the game, the children can use the information that they have learned about these characters to create a database that lists their characteristics, such as human, animal, male, female, real, fictional and so on. Alternatively, they can make a database first and then play the game to test their knowledge.

Differentiation
Choose easier characters for less able children to perform and to guess. Explain the game thoroughly to them and demonstrate a few character ideas, so that they know how the game works. Choose more difficult characters for more able children, to challenge their characterisation and improvisation skills, and their ability to guess.

The multimedia show

AGE RANGE 10–11

LEARNING OBJECTIVES
To create a multimedia presentation; to consider characterisation and dramatisation.

CURRICULUM LINKS
ICT KS1 and KS2: 2a, 2c, 3a, 3b, 4c, 5a.
QCA ICT: Unit 6A – Multimedia presentation.

What you need
Safe, open space.

What to do
● Ask the children to sit in a circle.
● Explain that they are going to be working on a multimedia presentation but without the use of real equipment.
● Ask the children to think about what 'multimedia' means and encourage them to give examples with their evidence. Multimedia can mean different kinds of media, for example, radio, newspapers and television. In computing terms, it refers to programs which combine text, image and sound.
● Divide the children into groups of five.
● Explain to the children that each group will be devising a multimedia news programme.
● Discuss how news programmes often use different media, for example, a studio-based presenter might link to reporters on location or by the use of video footage, or talk to guests via a radio link. Also, some reports on news programmes are presented using a multimedia program, for example, using tables and graphs to present facts and figures, and including sound effects or music, and images.
● Emphasise to the children that the programme has to be 'news worthy'. Encourage them to think of topics that they are going to cover, such as banning smoking in public places or allowing children to have free air travel if they are under the age of 12.
● Allow for 20 minutes of preparation time.
● Walk around the room, making sure that they are on the right track. Give help and advice where necessary and volunteer ideas if the children are having problems.
● Invite each group, in turn, to the front of the class to share their news programme.
● Allow constructive criticism from the rest of the class and ask the children which aspects of multimedia the performing group has used.

Differentiation
With less able children, make sure that they understand the term 'multimedia' and encourage them to work on linking different media together. More able children can develop this exercise to look at different types of programmes or subjects. An alternative to a news programme might be a drama-documentary or a reality show.

Drama and
Role-play

Choose your words

Our words

Our story

Who is in it? _____

_____

What is it about? _____

_____

_____

_____

_____